Our 50 ⭐ States

Our 50 ★ States

A FAMILY ADVENTURE ACROSS AMERICA

LYNNE CHENEY

ILLUSTRATED BY ROBIN PREISS GLASSER

Simon & Schuster Books for Young Readers
New York ★ London ★ Toronto ★ Sydney

One of the pleasures of my life has been sharing the beauty and variety of America with my grandchildren. I've ridden horseback with them in Grand Teton National Park, pulled crabs from the waters of Chesapeake Bay with them, walked with them on the Freedom Trail in Boston to see where Sam Adams and the Sons of Liberty plotted and planned for independence. But their father, my son-in-law, Phil Perry, has done most to increase their appreciation of our great country. A few years ago he drove my two older granddaughters, Kate and Elizabeth, then eight and five, from Washington, D.C., to Jackson, Wyoming, a trip that would normally take three days, but Phil, Kate, and Elizabeth took ten, following a circuitous route that allowed them to see everything from the National Baseball Hall of Fame, in Cooperstown, to the skyscraper canyons of Chicago to the great carvings of presidents Washington, Jefferson, Lincoln, and Theodore Roosevelt on Mount Rushmore.

My granddaughters' enthusiasm for all they saw and did inspired Robin Preiss Glasser and me to imagine the greatest family trip of all. What a wonder, we thought, to start in Massachusetts, where the Pilgrims landed; end in Hawaii, our newest state; and in between visit everything from the grasslands of Kentucky to the deserts of the American Southwest to the mountains of Alaska. Perhaps none of us will ever be lucky enough to take such a grand road trip, one in which we could hear the New York Philharmonic at Lincoln Center, the Preservation Hall Band in New Orleans, and mariachi music in Amarillo before we returned home, but surely we are fortunate to live in a country where all of these things—and so many more—form the fabric of our national life.

Lynne Cheney

To Kate, Elizabeth, Grace, Philip, and Richard Jonathan
—L. C.

For Bob, who is home to me
—R. P. G.

★ ACKNOWLEDGMENTS ★

Once again I have had the great good fortune to work with Robin Preiss Glasser, and I want to thank her for the inspiration she has provided all along the way. What a pleasure to work with someone who is not only a major talent, but a dear and life-affirming person.

My next thanks are to the American Enterprise Institute, which is so ably led by its president, Chris DeMuth, and where I have been fortunate to work with amazing research assistants. I'd like particularly to recognize Kathryn Duryea, who with keen intelligence, unwavering persistence, and a careful eye for detail, brought this book home. I'd also like to thank Kathryn's predecessor, the capable Elisabeth Irwin, for organizing the fifty separate state research projects that are the basis for this book, as well as for overseeing *Our 50 States* in its beginnings.

Jacqueline Preiss Weitzman, who has assisted Robin in her research, has brought energy, humor, and wisdom to this book, as she has to previous collaborations. Robin and I would also like to thank Carolyn Bracken for her assistance.

I owe a debt to a cadre of staff assistants and interns at AEI, beginning with Kate Campaigne and Elizabeth Donnan and including Amy Bastian, Kristina Blair, Irene Dokko, Betsy Duncan, Kim Ferguson, Jessica Orsulak, Liz Roby, Sarah Runnells, Ann Speidel, and Lisa Valentine. Working under the direction of Kathryn Duryea and Elisabeth Irwin, these young women have answered questions on matters ranging from snakes in Maine to observatories in Arizona, often by checking with leading experts. I would be remiss if I did not thank those experts, men and women all across the country who have responded with knowledge and patience to our queries.

Robin and I have been especially lucky to have the smart, compassionate, and visionary Paula Wiseman as our editor at Simon and Schuster and the talented and resourceful Dan Potash as our creative director. Indeed, I would like to thank the entire Simon and Schuster team for extraordinary support, beginning at the top with Jack Romanos, president and CEO; Rick Richter, president and publisher of the Children's Division; and Rubin Pfeffer, senior vice president and publisher of Children's Trade Publishing. Others to whom I am grateful are Lisa Ford, director of hardcover and paperback production, and Senior Managing Editor Dorothy Gribbin. Jessica Sonkin, Erica Stahler, Alexandra Penfold, Carol Chou, Michelle Montague, Jennifer Zatorski, and Karen Frangipane also played important roles, and I would like to thank them. I am also grateful to Lee Wade, Brenda Bowen, Hilary Goodman, and Tracy van Straaten.

I'd like to thank Washington attorney Robert Barnett for representing me on this book as on others. He has deep knowledge of the publishing industry, which is no small matter, but equally important are his enthusiasm and friendship.

★ CONTENTS ★

Emily Dickinson home

The Round Barn at the Shelburne Museum

Martin Luther King Jr.

Touro Synagogue

Alexander Calder Sculpture

Fort Kent

Carpenters' Hall

Grand Ole Opry

U.S. Marine Corps War Memorial

Samuel Wilson

George M. Cohan

Amelia Bloomer

Gettysburg memorial

Abraham Lincoln

U.S. Capitol

William Julius "Judy" Johnson

The Citadel

Statue of Liberty

Washington Monument

Fort Sumter

Ellis Island

Spirit of St. Louis

Susan B. Anthony

St. Joseph's Chapel

Cadillac

Benjamin Franklin

W.P. Snyder

Teddy bear

Harriet Tubman

Liberty Bell

Rita Moreno

The White House

Elvis Presley

Preservation Hall Jazz Band

Wienermobile

Epcot

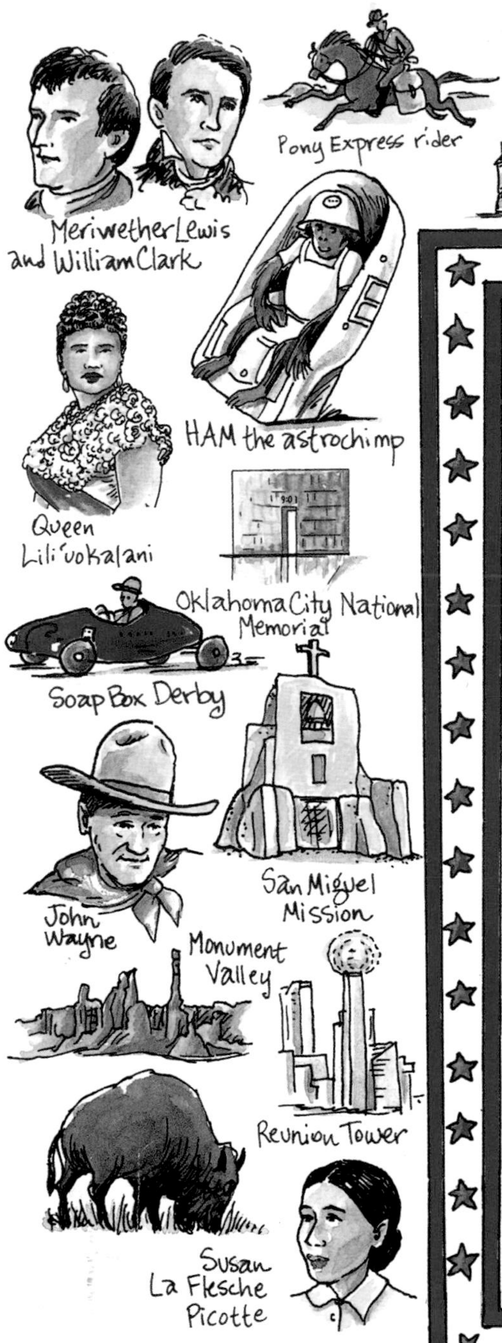

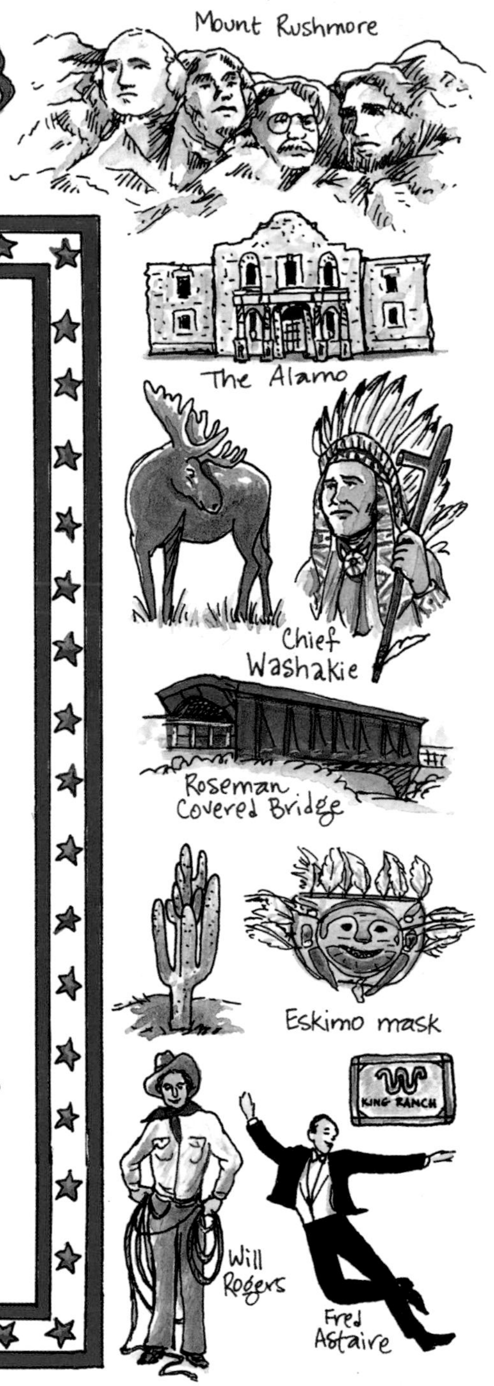

Meriwether Lewis and William Clark
Pony Express rider
HAM the astrochimp
Queen Lili'uokalani
Oklahoma City National Memorial
Soap Box Derby
John Wayne
San Miguel Mission
Monument Valley
Reunion Tower
Susan La Flesche Picotte

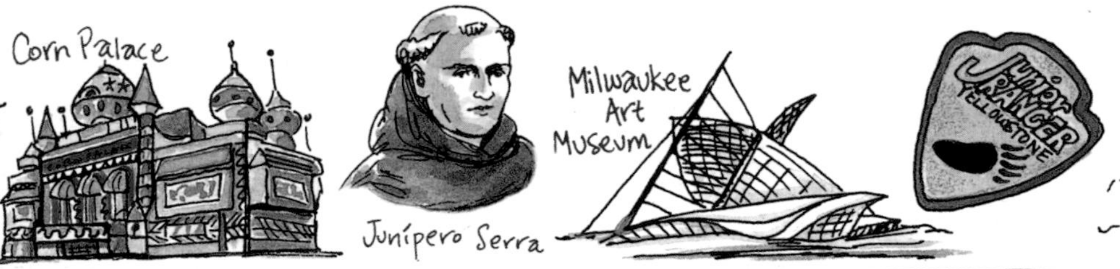

Corn Palace
Junípero Serra
Milwaukee Art Museum
JUNIOR RANGER
YELLOWSTONE

Mount Rushmore
The Alamo
Chief Washakie
Roseman Covered Bridge
Eskimo mask
KING RANCH
Will Rogers
Fred Astaire

TO
WEST
44A
NORTH
3
TO
EAST
44
"This land is your land,
this land is my land . . ."
PLYMOUTH ROCK
LANDING PLACE OF THE PILGRIMS
1620
COMMONWEALTH OF MASSACHUSETTS

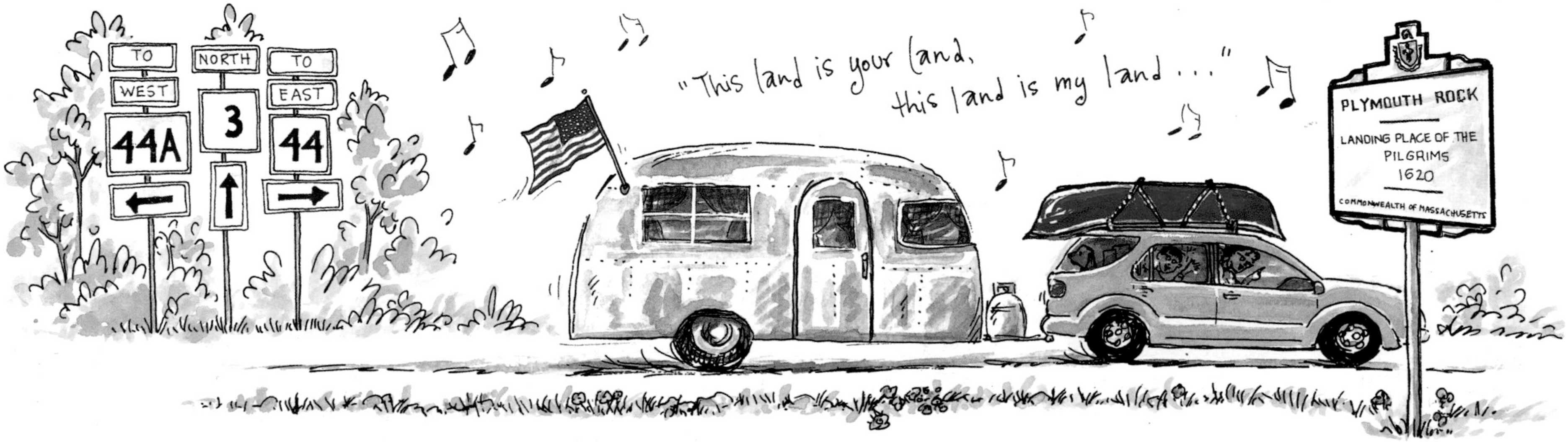

1621 1st Thanksgiving

1620 Mayflower Compact: Pilgrims' plan of government

1625: 1st apple orchard

1634: 1st public park: Boston Common

State motto: "By the sword we seek peace, but peace only under liberty."

1961 John F. Kennedy: nation's youngest elected president

Dear Grandma,
Cool foods I ate in Massachusetts: Boston cream pie (yum), Boston baked beans (good), cod (okay).
Love, Annie

The Hail to the Sunrise statue honors Indian nations.

Mohawk Trail

Dalton

Lenox

Tanglewood

The Berkshires

Holyoke

Connecticut River

IT HAPPENED HERE:
In April 1775, after the first shots of the Revolutionary War were fired at Lexington, Americans at Concord forced the British to retreat.

Concord

Minute Man National Historical Park

In this Amherst house Emily Dickinson wrote some of America's greatest poetry.

Amherst

Worcester

alex. i'm watching a guy make shoes in the 19th century. kidding! it's at old sturbridge village. ben

Sturbridge

1933 Frances Perkins: 1st woman Cabinet member

Naismith Memorial Basketball Hall of Fame, Springfield

Springfield

Families have long enjoyed listening to the music of the Boston Symphony Orchestra at Tanglewood.

Crane & Company, in Dalton, makes the paper for U.S. currency.

1926: Robert Goddard launches 1st liquid fuel rocket.

MASSACHUSETTS 1788

State bird: Black-capped chickadee

State flower: Mayflower

Dr. Seuss National Memorial, Springfield

Cranberry juice is the official beverage of Massachusetts.

Cranberry bogs

1903 1st baseball World Series opening games

1st subway 1898

1891: 1st basketball game

1846

1st lockstitch sewing machine patented

1843: John Manjiro, 1st Japanese to live in America, arrives in New Bedford.

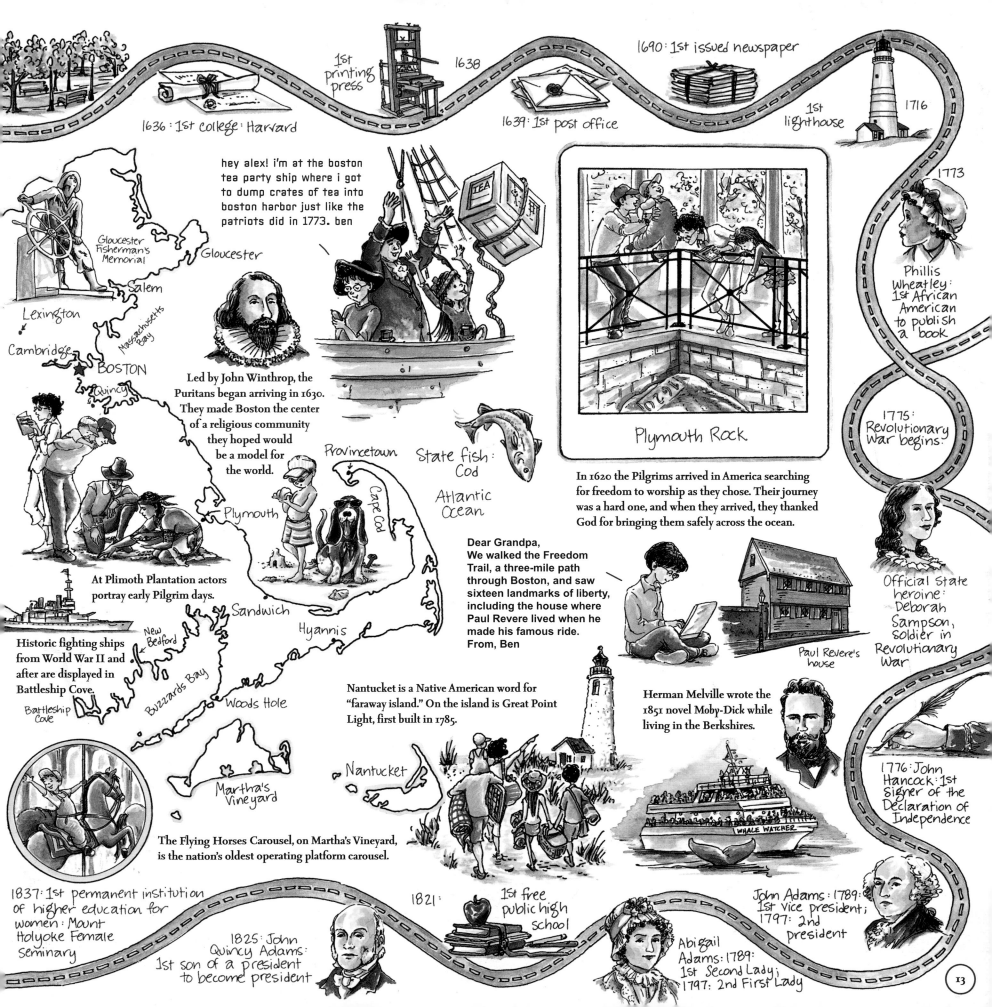

1636: 1st college: Harvard

1st printing press 1638

1639: 1st post office

1690: 1st issued newspaper

1st lighthouse 1716

hey alex! i'm at the boston tea party ship where i got to dump crates of tea into boston harbor just like the patriots did in 1773. ben

Led by John Winthrop, the Puritans began arriving in 1630. They made Boston the center of a religious community they hoped would be a model for the world.

Plymouth Rock

1773

Phillis Wheatley: 1st African American to publish a book

In 1620 the Pilgrims arrived in America searching for freedom to worship as they chose. Their journey was a hard one, and when they arrived, they thanked God for bringing them safely across the ocean.

1775: Revolutionary War begins.

State fish: Cod

Atlantic Ocean

At Plimoth Plantation actors portray early Pilgrim days.

Dear Grandpa,
We walked the Freedom Trail, a three-mile path through Boston, and saw sixteen landmarks of liberty, including the house where Paul Revere lived when he made his famous ride.
From, Ben

Paul Revere's house

Official State heroine: Deborah Sampson, soldier in Revolutionary War

Historic fighting ships from World War II and after are displayed in Battleship Cove.

Battleship Cove

Nantucket is a Native American word for "faraway island." On the island is Great Point Light, first built in 1785.

Herman Melville wrote the 1851 novel Moby-Dick while living in the Berkshires.

1776: John Hancock: 1st signer of the Declaration of Independence

WHALE WATCHER

The Flying Horses Carousel, on Martha's Vineyard, is the nation's oldest operating platform carousel.

1837: 1st permanent institution of higher education for women: Mount Holyoke Female Seminary

1825: John Quincy Adams: 1st son of a president to become president

1821: 1st free public high school

Abigail Adams: 1789: 1st Second Lady; 1797: 2nd First Lady

John Adams: 1789: 1st vice president; 1797: 2nd president

A bay and a river are named after the Penobscot Indians.

Shipbuilder George Bourne began decorating the Wedding Cake House in Kennebunk in 1855.

The Isaac H. Evans is one of the oldest surviving schooners in America.

Maine's Chester Greenwood designed the first earmuffs at age fifteen.

"Our search will be in vain, To find a fairer spot on earth Than Maine! Maine! Maine!"

Fort Kent

State bird: Black-capped chickadee

Maine has no poisonous snakes.

To restore puffin colonies in Maine, baby puffins have been transplanted to the state from Newfoundland, Canada.

Appalachian Mountains

Mount Katahdin

Rafting on the Penobscot River

Penobscot River

The Appalachian Trail begins at Mount Katahdin and extends all the way to Georgia.

The moose is a state symbol of Maine.

62-foot-tall statue in honor of Abnaki Indians

Skowhegan

Vienna

Paul Bunyan Statue

Bangor

Wild Blueberry Festival

Machias

AUGUSTA

Lobstering in Maine

More than 90 percent of the nation's lobster harvest comes from along the coast of Maine.

For many years Margaret Chase Smith, of Skowhegan, was the only woman in the U.S. Senate.

Old Fort Western, built 1754

New Gloucester

Brunswick

Bath

Portland

Penobscot Bay

Mt. Desert Island

Acadia National Park

Gulf of Maine

Kennebunk

York

Maine is the only state whose name has just one syllable.

hey alex! did you know that maine is the toothpick capital of the world? ben

Maine Maritime Museum, Bath

MAINE ★ STATEHOOD 1820

State flower: White pine cone and tassel

Maine has seventy-one lighthouses.

Born in Vienna, Maine, Milton Bradley founded the game company that makes Scrabble, the Game of Life, and Twister.

SCRABBLE

In 1851 Harriet Beecher Stowe wrote Uncle Tom's Cabin in Brunswick.

Civil War hero Joshua Chamberlain taught at Bowdoin College, in Brunswick.

Built in 1719 as a prison, the Old Gaol in York is today a museum.

Founded in 1783 by missionaries, the Sabbathday Lake Shaker Community, in New Gloucester, is the only active Shaker community today.

The state motto memorializes the words of Revolutionary War hero John Stark, of Manchester.

"Live free or die." State motto

Franklin Pierce, of Hillsborough, became the fourteenth president of the United States in 1853.

State bird: Purple finch

alex. i gave a dollar to a fund that will help people remember the old man of the mountain. ben

Camping in the White Mountains

At his farm in Franconia, Robert Frost wrote poems of New England life.

The highest wind speed ever recorded was on Mount Washington: 231 mph.

White Mountains

Franconia

Site of the former Old Man of the Mountain

Mount Washington

Mt. Washington Cog Railway

"Castle in the Clouds": hiking, waterfalls, views

Dartmouth College

Hanover

Christmas tree farms

Since 1920 New Hampshire has held the nation's first presidential primary.

Franklin

Lake Winnipesaukee

•Newport

CONCORD

Merrimack River

•Hillsborough

The Christa McAuliffe Planetarium, in Concord, honors the astronaut who was a teacher.

Samuel Wilson, of Mason, became known as Uncle Sam during the War of 1812.

•Manchester

Atlantic Ocean

Mason.

•Nashua

★ NEW HAMPSHIRE ★

1788

State flower: Purple lilac

Daniel Webster, born in Franklin in 1782, became a lawyer, orator, and statesman.

The Old Man of the Mountain was a favorite New Hampshire landmark until the granite forming the face fell from the mountain in 2003.

In 1830 author and journalist Sarah Josepha Hale, of Newport, wrote the poem known today as "Mary Had a Little Lamb."

"I love Vermont because of her hills and valleys, her scenery and invigorating climate, but most of all, I love her because of her indomitable people." ~ Calvin Coolidge

Chester A. Arthur, of Fairfield, became the twenty-first president in 1881.

Granite, marble, and slate are Vermont's official rocks.

Vice President Calvin Coolidge was at his family's farm in Plymouth Notch in 1923 when he received word that President Warren G. Harding had died. His father, a notary public, swore him in by kerosene lamplight as our thirtieth president.

Fairfield

dairy

Ski gondolas

Stowe is one of Vermont's many popular ski resorts.

Burlington

The Round Barn at the Shelburne Museum

Shelburne

Stowe

Waterbury

MONTPELIER

alex. it takes about 35 gallons of sap — to make 1 gallon of maple syrup. that's a lotta sap. ben

Ben & Jerry's Ice Cream Factory

Lake Champlain is named for French explorer Samuel de Champlain, who entered the lake by canoe in 1609. He reported "many rivers falling into the lake" and "a great abundance of fish."

Vermont was an independent republic from 1777 to 1791.

In 1814 Emma Willard opened higher education to women at the Middlebury Female Seminary.

Middlebury

Green Mountain National Forest

In 1836 Alexander Twilight became the first African American to serve in the Vermont state legislature.

Sugar maple trees produce beautiful leaves in the fall and sap for maple syrup in early spring.

The Ticonderoga

Ethan Allen and the Green Mountain Boys fought for the rights of Vermonters and joined the patriot cause in the Revolutionary War.

IT HAPPENED HERE: The Green Mountain Boys helped win the Battle of Bennington in 1777. The battlefield is in New York.

← Plymouth

Healdville

Crowley Cheese Factory: oldest in America

VERMONT
STATEHOOD 1791
Sugarhouse

State bird: Hermit thrush
State flower: Red clover

The Shelburne Museum, which looks like a nineteenth-century New England town, is home to the steamboat Ticonderoga.

Bennington
Bennington Battle Monument

Brattleboro

Grandma Moses Gallery and Schoolhouse honor the painter's life and work.

Vermont has more than one hundred covered bridges.

The Charlotte whale, a fossil more than ten thousand years old, was found by railroad workers in 1849 more than 150 miles from any ocean.

State animal: Morgan horse

Samuel Slater, who brought knowledge of the Industrial Revolution to America, built a water-powered textile mill in Pawtucket in 1793.

State rock: Cumberlandite
This rock attracts magnets and is about 1½ billion years old.

In 1952 a company in Pawtucket began manufacturing Mr. Potato Head, the creation of George Lerner.

Gilbert Stuart, born in Rhode Island, painted the portrait of George Washington that is on the dollar bill.

George M. Cohan, of Providence, could sing, act, and dance. The 1942 movie Yankee Doodle Dandy is the story of his life.

The first Baptist church in America was formed by Roger Williams in 1638. This Providence building was completed in 1775.

Bristol is home to the oldest continuous 4th of July parade. It began in 1785.

Jews fleeing religious persecution built the Touro Synagogue. Dedicated in 1763 and located in Newport, it is the oldest synagogue in the United States.

A dome in the Jamestown windmill, built in 1787, rotates so that the arms face the wind.

The first circus in America was in Newport in 1774.

State flower:
Violet

alex. there are giant green animals in portsmouth. they're topiary, or sculptured bushes. ben

Green Animals Topiary Garden

"The Sailing Capital of America"

The three-and-a-half-mile Cliff Walk offers spectacular views of the ocean and of Newport's nineteenth-century mansions.

Block Island

Block Island Sound

Dear Grandma, Did you ever eat a "stuffie"? It's baked quahog, which is clams. Love, Annie

State bird:
Rhode Island Red

Rhode Island, the smallest state, has the longest official name: the State of Rhode Island and Providence Plantations.

The International Quahog Bake-off Amateur level

QUAHOG 1st Place!!

Quahog Festival, Wickford

Slatersville · Woonsocket
Blackstone River
Jerimoth Hill
Pawtucket
PROVIDENCE
Cranston
Warwick
Narragansett Bay
Bristol
Portsmouth
Wickford
Aquidneck Island
Jamestown
Newport

RHODE ISLAND
1790

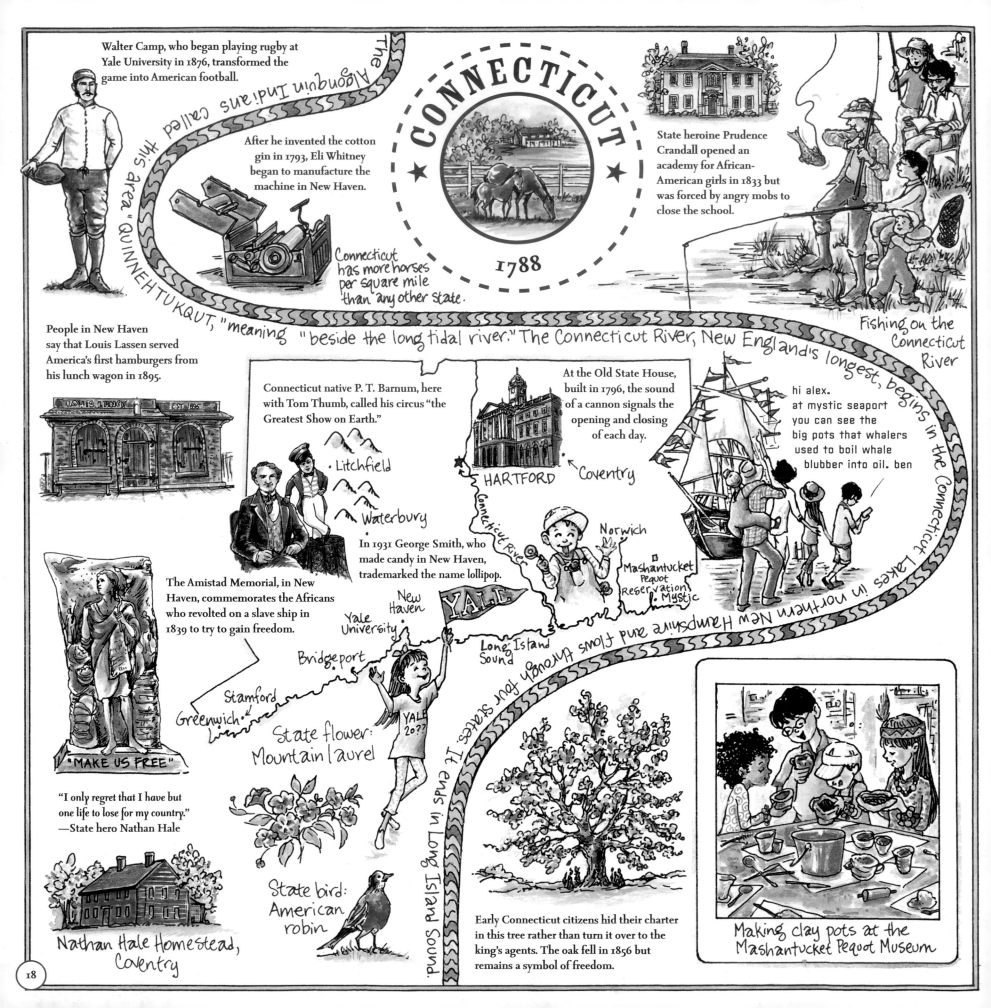

Walter Camp, who began playing rugby at Yale University in 1876, transformed the game into American football.

The Algonquin Indians called this area "QUINNEHTUKQUT," meaning "beside the long tidal river." The Connecticut River, New England's longest, begins in the Connecticut Lakes in northern New Hampshire, flows through four states. It ends in Long Island Sound.

After he invented the cotton gin in 1793, Eli Whitney began to manufacture the machine in New Haven.

CONNECTICUT
1788

Connecticut has more horses per square mile than any other state.

State heroine Prudence Crandall opened an academy for African-American girls in 1833 but was forced by angry mobs to close the school.

Fishing on the Connecticut River

People in New Haven say that Louis Lassen served America's first hamburgers from his lunch wagon in 1895.

LOUIS LUNCH EST. 1895

Connecticut native P. T. Barnum, here with Tom Thumb, called his circus "the Greatest Show on Earth."

• Litchfield

Waterbury

In 1931 George Smith, who made candy in New Haven, trademarked the name lollipop.

At the Old State House, built in 1796, the sound of a cannon signals the opening and closing of each day.

HARTFORD   ← Coventry

hi alex.
at mystic seaport you can see the big pots that whalers used to boil whale blubber into oil. ben

Norwich

Mashantucket Pequot Reservation
• Mystic

The Amistad Memorial, in New Haven, commemorates the Africans who revolted on a slave ship in 1839 to try to gain freedom.

"MAKE US FREE"

New Haven

Yale University •

Bridgeport

Stamford

Greenwich

YALE

YALE 20??

Long Island Sound

State flower: Mountain laurel

"I only regret that I have but one life to lose for my country."
—State hero Nathan Hale

State bird: American robin

Nathan Hale Homestead, Coventry

Early Connecticut citizens hid their charter in this tree rather than turn it over to the king's agents. The oak fell in 1856 but remains a symbol of freedom.

Making clay pots at the Mashantucket Pequot Museum

alex. rest stops on the new jersey turnpike are named for famous new jerseyans. bet you don't know who richard stockton is. ben

New Jersey is the most densely populated state.

In 1825 John Stevens, of Hoboken, was the first to build a steam locomotive in America.

STEEL PIER HIGH-DIVING HORSES

Dear Grandma, We're at the Joyce Kilmer rest stop. He wrote, "I think I shall never see A poem lovely as a tree." Love, Annie

High Point

Kittatinny Mountain

In Menlo Park, Thomas Edison invented the phonograph and the first practical lightbulb.

Paterson

Newark

Hoboken

Jersey City

Menlo Park

The first movies were made in New Jersey.

Princeton University

Princeton

TRENTON

Molly Pitcher: Revolutionary War heroine

Atlantic City's famous boardwalk was built in 1870. Early visitors could see fortune-tellers, snake charmers, and a woman on horseback diving forty feet from a tower into a pool. Saltwater taffy, popular then, is still a favorite today.

IT HAPPENED HERE: In 1776 George Washington crossed the Delaware River, won the Battle of Trenton, and changed the course of history.

Condensed soup began in Camden in 1897.

TOMATO SOUP

Fralinger's Original SALT WATER TAFFY

BERKELEY'S

Dotty's Nut World

State flower:

Violet

Atlantic City

State bird:

Eastern goldfinch

★ NEW JERSEY ★

1787

Delaware River

Camden

Haddonfield

In 1858 the first dinosaur skeleton was discovered in Haddonfield.

Atlantic City

Ocean City

Atlantic City

Atlantic Ocean

Cape May

FAMOUS NEW JERSEYANS

Cape May is known as one of the "Prettiest Painted Places in America" because of the hundreds of restored Victorian homes there.

Paul Robeson, singer and actor (1898–1976)

Count Basie, jazz musician (1904–1984)

Grover Cleveland, president (1837–1908)

Dorothea Lange, photographer (1895–1965)

Frank Sinatra, entertainer (1915–1998)

Thomas Edison, inventor (1847–1931)

Stephen Crane, author (1871–1900)

Albert Einstein, physicist (1879–1955)

Richard Stockton, signer, Declaration of Independence (1730–1781)

Mary Mapes Dodge, children's author (1831–1905)

Alice Paul, suffragist (1885–1977)

Virginia Apgar, doctor (1909–1974)

19

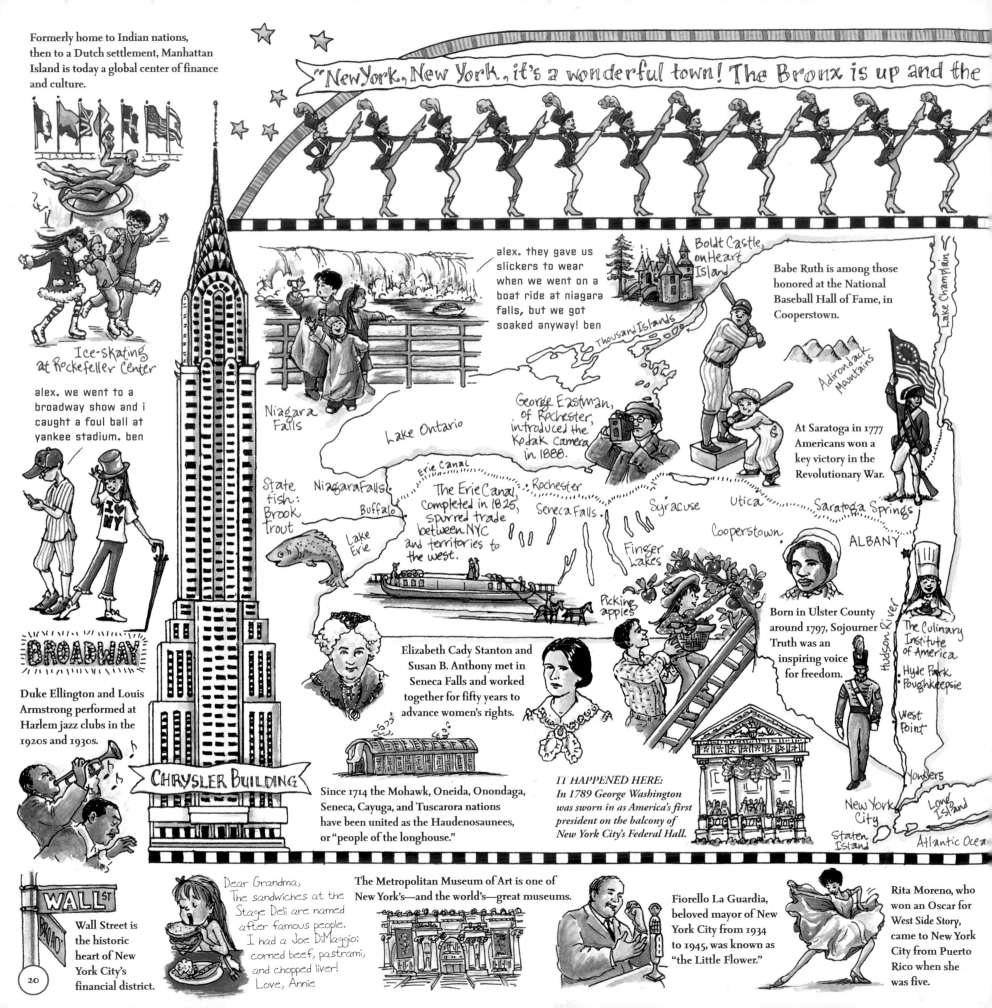

Formerly home to Indian nations, then to a Dutch settlement, Manhattan Island is today a global center of finance and culture.

Ice-Skating at Rockefeller Center

alex. we went to a broadway show and i caught a foul ball at yankee stadium. ben

BROADWAY

Duke Ellington and Louis Armstrong performed at Harlem jazz clubs in the 1920s and 1930s.

CHRYSLER BUILDING

alex. they gave us slickers to wear when we went on a boat ride at niagara falls, but we got soaked anyway! ben

Niagara Falls

State fish: Brook trout

Lake Ontario

Erie Canal

Niagara Falls

Buffalo

Lake Erie

The Erie Canal, completed in 1825, spurred trade between NYC and territories to the west.

Rochester

Seneca Falls

George Eastman, of Rochester, introduced the Kodak camera in 1888.

Boldt Castle, on Heart Island

Thousand Islands

Babe Ruth is among those honored at the National Baseball Hall of Fame, in Cooperstown.

Adirondack Mountains

Lake Champlain

At Saratoga in 1777 Americans won a key victory in the Revolutionary War.

Syracuse

Utica

Saratoga Springs

Finger Lakes

Cooperstown

ALBANY

Picking apples

Elizabeth Cady Stanton and Susan B. Anthony met in Seneca Falls and worked together for fifty years to advance women's rights.

Born in Ulster County around 1797, Sojourner Truth was an inspiring voice for freedom.

Hudson River

The Culinary Institute of America

Hyde Park
Poughkeepsie

West Point

Yonkers

New York City

Staten Island

Long Island

Atlantic Ocean

Since 1714 the Mohawk, Oneida, Onondaga, Seneca, Cayuga, and Tuscarora nations have been united as the Haudenosaunees, or "people of the longhouse."

IT HAPPENED HERE: In 1789 George Washington was sworn in as America's first president on the balcony of New York City's Federal Hall.

WALL ST

BROAD

Wall Street is the historic heart of New York City's financial district.

Dear Grandma, The sandwiches at the Stage Deli are named after famous people. I had a Joe DiMaggio: corned beef, pastrami, and chopped liver! Love, Annie

The Metropolitan Museum of Art is one of New York's—and the world's—great museums.

Fiorello La Guardia, beloved mayor of New York City from 1934 to 1945, was known as "the Little Flower."

Rita Moreno, who won an Oscar for West Side Story, came to New York City from Puerto Rico when she was five.

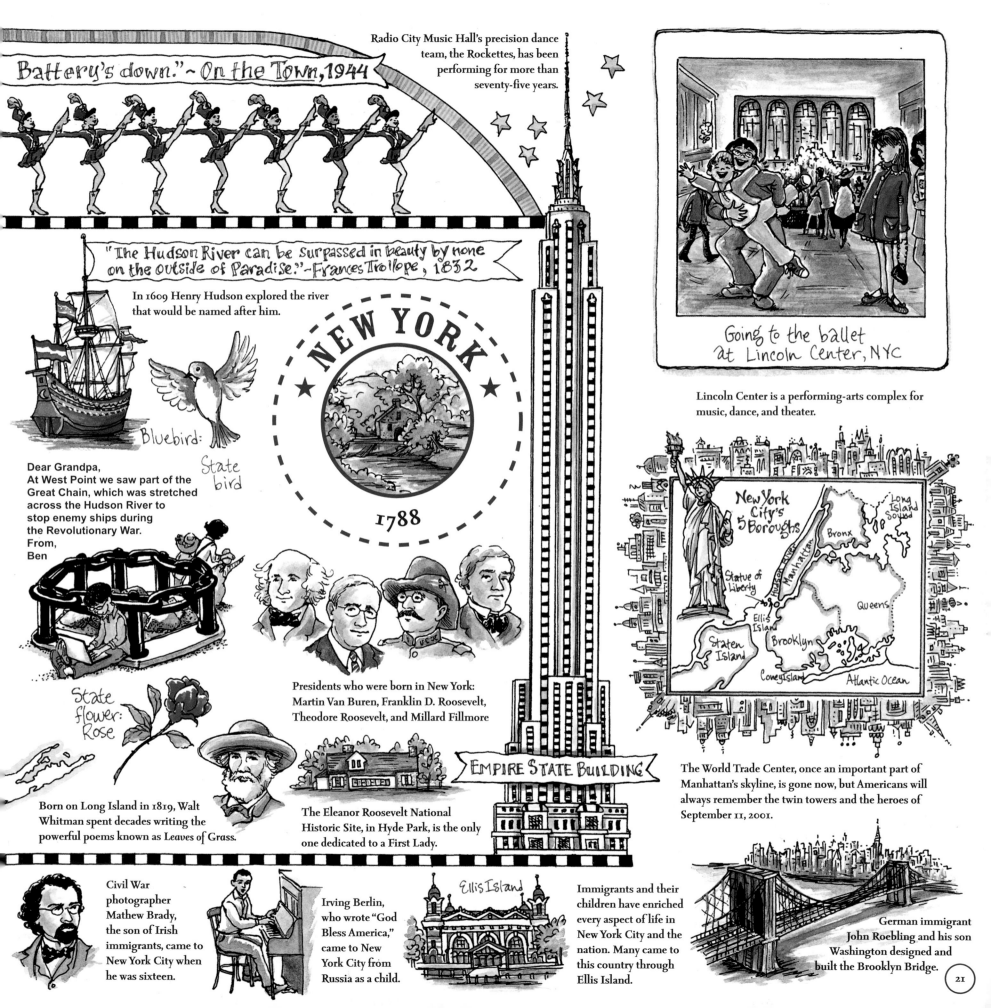

"Battery's down." ~ *On the Town*, 1944

Radio City Music Hall's precision dance team, the Rockettes, has been performing for more than seventy-five years.

Going to the ballet at Lincoln Center, NYC

Lincoln Center is a performing-arts complex for music, dance, and theater.

"The Hudson River can be surpassed in beauty by none on the outside of Paradise." ~ Frances Trollope, 1832

In 1609 Henry Hudson explored the river that would be named after him.

Bluebird: State bird

NEW YORK
★ 1788 ★

Dear Grandpa,
At West Point we saw part of the Great Chain, which was stretched across the Hudson River to stop enemy ships during the Revolutionary War.
From,
Ben

State flower: Rose

Born on Long Island in 1819, Walt Whitman spent decades writing the powerful poems known as *Leaves of Grass*.

Presidents who were born in New York: Martin Van Buren, Franklin D. Roosevelt, Theodore Roosevelt, and Millard Fillmore

The Eleanor Roosevelt National Historic Site, in Hyde Park, is the only one dedicated to a First Lady.

EMPIRE STATE BUILDING

New York City's 5 Boroughs
Statue of Liberty
Ellis Island
Staten Island
Coney Island
Manhattan
Hudson River
Bronx
Long Island Sound
Queens
Brooklyn
Atlantic Ocean

The World Trade Center, once an important part of Manhattan's skyline, is gone now, but Americans will always remember the twin towers and the heroes of September 11, 2001.

Civil War photographer Mathew Brady, the son of Irish immigrants, came to New York City when he was sixteen.

Irving Berlin, who wrote "God Bless America," came to New York City from Russia as a child.

Ellis Island

Immigrants and their children have enriched every aspect of life in New York City and the nation. Many came to this country through Ellis Island.

German immigrant John Roebling and his son Washington designed and built the Brooklyn Bridge.

1681: Quaker William Penn receives a land grant from Charles II; the new colony is to be called Pennsylvania, in honor of his father.

1682: The General Assembly of Pennsylvania adopts the Great Law, which reflects Penn's belief in religious freedom.

1st seal of Pennsylvania

1790–1800: With the Constitution ratified, Philadelphia becomes the U.S. capital for ten years.

State motto: "Virtue, liberty, and independence."

Fifteenth president James Buchanan was born in 1791 in Cove Gap.

Oliver Hazard Perry commanded a fleet of ships that defeated the British on Lake Erie during the War of 1812.

Lake Erie

In 1859 Edwin Drake struck oil in Titusville and launched an industry.

State animal: Whitetail deer

Titusville

Allegheny National Forest

Thousands of people go to Gobbler's Knob each year on February 2, Groundhog Day, to observe whether Punxsutawney Phil sees his shadow.

Punxsutawney

Three rivers—the Ohio, the Monongahela, and the Allegheny—come together at Pittsburgh.

Pittsburgh

After making a fortune in the steel industry, centered in Pittsburgh, Scottish immigrant Andrew Carnegie gave millions away.

Cove Gap

Gettysburg

1787: In Philadelphia's State House (today Independence Hall), the U.S. Constitution is drafted. Gen. George Washington presides.

The greatest battle of the Civil War occurred at Gettysburg in 1863. Afterward, in the Gettysburg Address, Abraham Lincoln honored those who had died.

Pittsburgh native Martha Graham transformed the art of dance.

State bird: Ruffed grouse

Born in 1898 in Lawnton, now part of Philadelphia, Alexander Calder is best known for his invention of the mobile.

Treaty of Paris officially ends Revolutionary War. 1783

September 1777–May 1778: The British occupy Philadelphia; they leave when France agrees to help the Americans seeking independence.

1776–1783: Philadelphian Robert Morris, a signer of the Declaration of Independence, organized financing for the American Revolution.

1700s:
Philadelphia attracts a diverse population and soon becomes a political, commercial, and cultural center.

1752:
Benjamin Franklin, a Philadelphian since 1723, demonstrates that lightning is electricity.

1765:
The British impose the Stamp Act, taxing colonists. Philadelphians protest.

State flower: Mountain laurel

Marian Anderson, of Philadelphia, was the first African American to sing with the Metropolitan Opera in New York City.

Dear Grandpa,
Mom got a quilt at the Lancaster farmers' market in Pennsylvania Dutch country, and I ate shoofly pie!
From, Ben

1774:
The First Continental Congress meets in Philadelphia's Carpenters' Hall; it addresses grievances against England.

Free Africans established the Mother Bethel Church in 1791.

★ PENNSYLVANIA ★
1787

Scranton

Pocono Mountains

Delaware Water Gap National Recreation Area

George Washington's headquarters at Valley Forge

Washington Crossing Historic Park

HARRISBURG
Hershey
Susquehanna River
Lancaster
Chadds Ford
Philadelphia
Valley Forge
Delaware River
• Gettysburg

In 1777–78 George Washington and his army endured a harsh winter at Valley Forge.

alex. eating a philadelphia cheesesteak on a cobblestone street makes me feel very philly! ben

Carpenters' Hall

Dear Grandma,
I want to LIVE in Hershey, PA—the air smells like chocolate, and even the streetlights are shaped like Hershey's Kisses!
Love and Annie

Paintings by three generations of the Wyeth family hang in the Brandywine River Museum, in Chadds Ford.

Pennsylvania ranks first in the nation in mushroom production.

July 4, 1776:
The Second Continental Congress adopts the Declaration of Independence; members, including Benjamin Franklin, begin signing in August.

October 1776:
Appointed by Congress as a commissioner to France, Benjamin Franklin leaves for Paris.

July 8, 1776:
For the first public reading of the Declaration of Independence, the Liberty Bell is rung, according to legend.

Inkstand used to sign Declaration of Independence

Baseball Hall of Famer William Julius "Judy" Johnson grew up in Wilmington and played for the Negro Leagues in the 1920s and 1930s.

In July 1776 Caesar Rodney, of Dover, rode eighty miles to Philadelphia through rain and thunder to cast the deciding vote for American independence.

Delaware Memorial Bridge is the longest twin span suspension bridge.

Winterthur Museum and Garden

Brandywine Creek

Wilmington

Newark

Thomas Garrett's home in Wilmington was a refuge on the Underground Railroad. He helped more than 2,700 people escape from slavery.

Swedish settlers, who began to arrive in 1638, brought the log cabin to America.

Pea Patch Island

Legend has it that Pea Patch Island was created when a ship carrying peas hit a mud bank. The peas grew into plants, giving the island its name.

DELAWARE

1787

"Then join hand in hand, brave Americans all! By uniting we stand, by dividing we fall!"
—John Dickinson, "The Liberty Song"

John Dickinson Plantation

In 1787 John Dickinson, who grew up near Dover, represented Delaware at the Constitutional Convention.

Annie Jump Cannon, born in Dover, classified some 350,000 stars.

State flower: Peach blossom

DOVER

Delaware Bay

State bird: Blue hen

guess what, alex? horseshoe crabs aren't really crabs, but ancient animals that have been around more than 400 million years! ben

Dear Grandpa,
Dad brought us to play in Enchanted Woods while Mom tours the Winterthur mansion, where some of the Du Ponts lived. Yesterday we went to Punkin Chunkin, a contest that started with people throwing pumpkins. Now they bring air cannons and shoot the pumpkins nearly a mile! Franklin hid in the camper.
From, Ben

Eleuthère Irénée du Pont, who came to the United States from France in 1800, started the DuPont company and established an important Delaware family.

In 1631 a Dutch colony called Zwaanendael, meaning "Valley of the Swans," was founded.

The Zwaanendael Museum

Lewes

The first bathing beauty contest was held at Rehoboth Beach in 1880. Thomas Edison was one of the three judges.

Rehoboth Beach

The Nanticoke Indian Powwow is an annual fall festival held near Millsboro.

Indian River Bay

Millsboro

State insect: Ladybug

State tree: American holly

Fenwick Island

Enchanted Woods, Winterthur Museum and Garden

Osprey

American bald eagle

Turkey vulture

Great egret

Canada geese

Tundra Swan

Great blue heron

Mallard

Snow goose

Delmarva fox squirrel

Forster's tern

Blue-winged teal

Diamondback terrapin

Raccoon

Baltimore checkerspot

Under a royal grant made to his father, the second Lord Baltimore established Maryland as a place where Catholics could worship, but the colony attracted even more Protestants. In 1649 a law was passed permitting both groups freedom of religion.

Mason-Dixon Line

"O'er the land of the free and the home of the brave."
— Francis Scott Key

IT HAPPENED HERE:
Francis Scott Key wrote "The Star-Spangled Banner" after watching the bombardment of Fort McHenry during the Battle of Baltimore in the War of 1812.

Baltimore

Columbia

Silver Spring

ANNAPOLIS

Chesapeake Bay Bridge

Easton

Chesapeake Bay

Blackwater National Wildlife Refuge

Potomac River

St. Marys City

Ocean City

Assateague Island

Dear Grandpa,
We've seen amazing wild birds at Blackwater National Wildlife Refuge— Canada geese and tundra swans, but the most awesome were actual American bald eagles!
Annie is practicing her duck calls for the World Championship Live Duck Calling Contest in Easton, but I don't think she's going to win.
From, Ben

State bird: Baltimore oriole

State flower: Black-eyed susan

In 1829 construction began on the Baltimore and Ohio Railroad, the first public railroad in the nation.

UNITED STATES NAVAL ACADEMY FOUNDED 1845

The U.S. Naval Academy, at Annapolis, has trained midshipmen since 1845.

Wild ponies live on Assateague Island.

Harriet Tubman: After escaping from slavery in 1849, she then helped others escape.

National Aquarium, Baltimore

MARYLAND
Blue crab
1788

The first colonists arrived aboard the Ark and Dove in 1634. They founded St. Marys City.

Frederick Douglass: Having escaped from slavery in 1838, he became a spokesman for freedom.

alex. on the uss constellation, in baltimore's inner harbor, i found out that in the civil war, 14-year-olds could be sailors. ben

25

George Washington
1732-1799
1st president

Mount Vernon, near Alexandria, was George Washington's beloved home.

Thomas Jefferson
1743-1826
3rd president

Monticello, near Charlottesville, is the home Thomas Jefferson designed for himself.

James Madison
1751-1836
4th president

State flower: Dogwood

State bird: Cardinal

VIRGINIA
★ ★
Jamestown Settlement
1788

In 1607 Jamestown, the first permanent English settlement in the New World, was founded.

The Pentagon is in Arlington.

The Iwo Jima Memorial in Arlington honors marine bravery in World War II.

The Tomb of the Unknowns at Arlington National Cemetery honors those who have died fighting for America.

Virginia is the birthplace of eight presidents, though three have other connections: William Henry Harrison to the Indiana Territory and Ohio, Woodrow Wilson to New Jersey, and Zachary Taylor to Kentucky.

Blue Ridge Mountains
Arlington
Alexandria
Orange
Charlottesville
Lexington
RICHMOND
Potomac River
Chesapeake Bay
Williamsburg
Jamestown
Hampton
Newport News
Norfolk
Appomattox Court House
Yorktown
Virginia Beach
Atlantic Ocean

Tennis great Arthur Ashe is honored in his hometown of Richmond.

Montpelier, near Orange, was home to James Madison and his family.

Woodrow Wilson
1856-1924
28th President

Gen. Robert E. Lee is buried in a chapel in Lexington. His favorite horse, Traveller, is buried outside the building.

James Monroe
1758-1831
5th president

Colonial Williamsburg

IT HAPPENED HERE:
In 1781, at Yorktown, George Washington defeated Gen. Charles Cornwallis. America became an independent nation.

Dear Grandpa,
At Williamsburg actors play colonial people, including those who were slaves. One told us how hard slave life was.
From, Ben

alex. at colonial williamsburg we learned how wigs were made in the olden days. ben

Dear Grandma,
The state dance of Virginia is the square dance.
Love, Annie

Entertainers Ella Fitzgerald and Pearl Bailey were both born in Newport News.

In 1775, at St. John's Church in Richmond, Patrick Henry said, "Give me liberty or give me death!"

In the McLean House in the village of Appomattox Court House, Confederate general Robert E. Lee surrendered to Union general Ulysses S. Grant in 1865.

Zachary Taylor
1784-1850
12th President

Hampton University was one of the first African-American colleges in the country. Noted educator Booker T. Washington went to school there.

John Tyler
1790-1862
10th President

The University of Virginia, in Charlottesville, was one of Thomas Jefferson's proudest achievements.

William Henry Harrison
1773-1841
9th president

In 1790, as the result of a bargain that Thomas Jefferson brokered, the nation's capital was located on the Potomac River: George Washington picked the exact site; Pierre L'Enfant, who fought in the Revolutionary War, designed the city; and Benjamin Banneker, a free black, did most of the surveying for it. In 1800 our national government began operating from the Federal City.

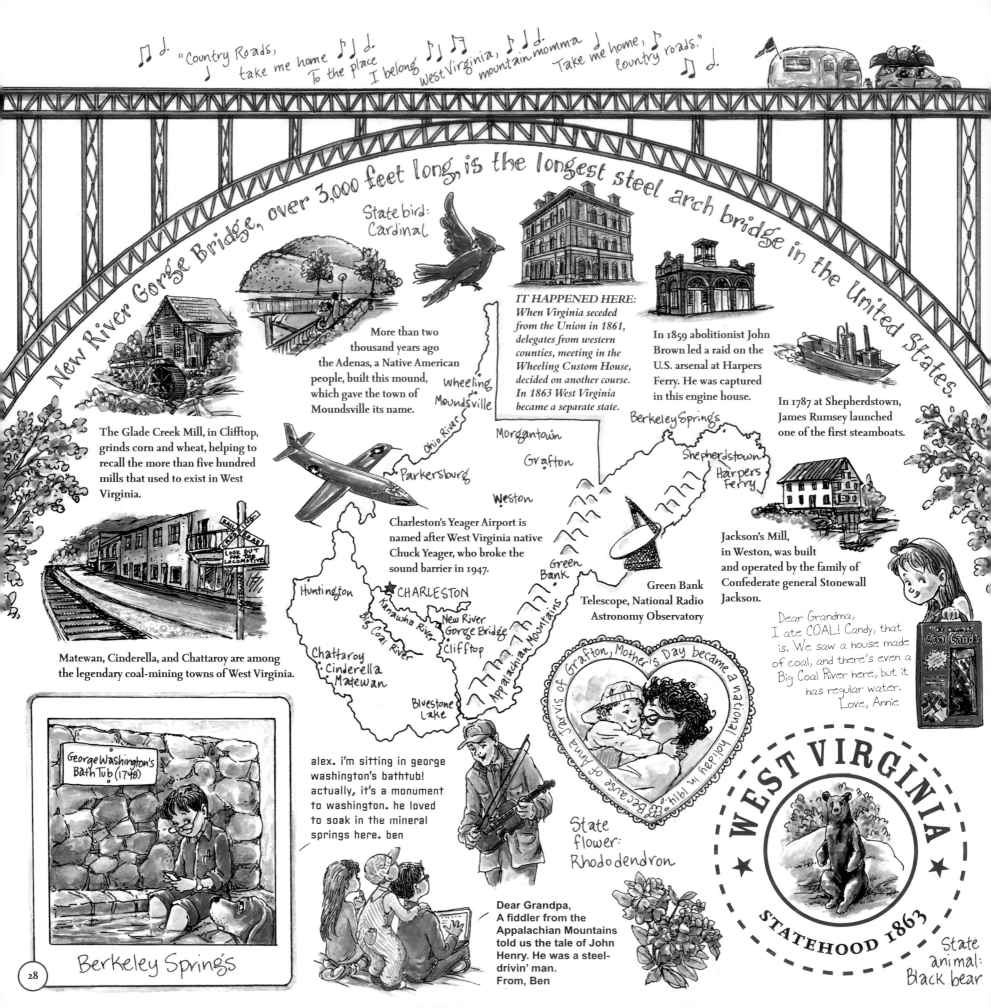

♫ ♩ "Country Roads, take me home ♪♪ ♩. To the place ♪ I belong ♫ ♪♫ West Virginia, ♪♪♩. mountain momma ♪ Take me home, ♪ country roads." ♫ ♩.

New River Gorge Bridge, over 3,000 feet long, is the longest steel arch bridge in the United States.

State bird: Cardinal

The Glade Creek Mill, in Clifftop, grinds corn and wheat, helping to recall the more than five hundred mills that used to exist in West Virginia.

More than two thousand years ago the Adenas, a Native American people, built this mound, which gave the town of Moundsville its name.

IT HAPPENED HERE: When Virginia seceded from the Union in 1861, delegates from western counties, meeting in the Wheeling Custom House, decided on another course. In 1863 West Virginia became a separate state.

In 1859 abolitionist John Brown led a raid on the U.S. arsenal at Harpers Ferry. He was captured in this engine house.

In 1787 at Shepherdstown, James Rumsey launched one of the first steamboats.

Matewan, Cinderella, and Chattaroy are among the legendary coal-mining towns of West Virginia.

Charleston's Yeager Airport is named after West Virginia native Chuck Yeager, who broke the sound barrier in 1947.

Green Bank Telescope, National Radio Astronomy Observatory

Jackson's Mill, in Weston, was built and operated by the family of Confederate general Stonewall Jackson.

Wheeling
Moundsville
Ohio River
Morgantown
Grafton
Parkersburg
Weston
Huntington
CHARLESTON
Kanawha River
Big Coal River
New River Gorge Bridge
Clifftop
Chattaroy
Cinderella
Matewan
Bluestone Lake
Appalachian Mountains
Green Bank
Berkeley Springs
Shepherdstown
Harpers Ferry

Dear Grandma,
I ate COAL! Candy, that is. We saw a house made of coal, and there's even a Big Coal River here, but it has regular water.
Love, Annie

The Original Coal Candy

George Washington's Bath Tub (1748)

Berkeley Springs

alex. i'm sitting in george washington's bathtub! actually, it's a monument to washington. he loved to soak in the mineral springs here. ben

Because of Anna Jarvis of Grafton, Mother's Day became a national holiday in 1914.

State flower: Rhododendron

Dear Grandpa,
A fiddler from the Appalachian Mountains told us the tale of John Henry. He was a steel-drivin' man.
From, Ben

WEST VIRGINIA
★ STATEHOOD 1863 ★

State animal: Black bear

State flower: Dogwood

State bird: Cardinal

"America...is a fabulous country...where miracles not only happen, but where they happen all the time."—North Carolina native Thomas Wolfe

NORTH CAROLINA
Chimney Rock
1789

Grandfather Mountain

alex. annie wouldn't walk across mile high swinging bridge on grandfather mountain, but i did and it was cool! ben

First Lady Dolley Madison, evangelist Billy Graham, and saxophonist John Coltrane were all born in North Carolina.

IT HAPPENED HERE: In 1960 in Greensboro, African-American students sat at a whites-only lunch counter and started a movement opposing segregation.

The Venus flytrap, a carnivorous plant, grows around Hampstead.

During the Civil War about 125,000 North Carolina men fought for the South and about 15,000 for the North.

Grandfather Mountain
Old Salem
Winston-Salem
Greensboro
Great Smoky Mountains
Asheville
Cherokee
Chimney Rock
Shelby
Charlotte
BLUE DEVILS DUKE
UNC TAR HEELS
UNC..DUKE
★ RALEIGH
Roanoke Island
Kitty Hawk
Cape Hatteras
Outer Banks
Ocracoke Island
Cape Lookout
Atlantic Ocean
Hampstead
Cape Fear

Just eight miles apart, Duke University and the University of North Carolina at Chapel Hill have an intense basketball rivalry.

In 1903 at Kill Devil Hill, near Kitty Hawk, brothers Orville and Wilbur Wright flew the first successful airplane.

The career of Blackbeard, a legendary pirate, came to an end near Ocracoke Island in 1718.

George Vanderbilt started building Asheville's Biltmore Estate, the nation's largest private house, in 1889.

In 1838, when the U.S. government forced them on a long march west, some one thousand Cherokees escaped the forced relocation. Their descendants demonstrate Cherokee culture at the Oconaluftee Indian Village, in Cherokee.

The banjo-playing style of Earl Scruggs, born near Shelby, created a distinctive bluegrass sound.

Dear Grandma, I had the best cake ever at Old Salem, which is a restored Moravian town. They make their cakes just like the Moravians used to—with potatoes! Love, Annie

North Carolina is a major supplier of the nation's tobacco, textiles, and turkeys.

Rainbow Row, Charleston

The loggerhead sea turtle, South Carolina's state reptile, can weigh up to four hundred pounds and live for eighty years.

Dear Grandpa,
At Swan Lake–Iris Gardens in Sumter they have eight species of swans from around the world.
From, Ben

Cowpens National Battlefield

King's Mountain National Military Park

Gaffney

Greenville

In 1964 Charles Townes, of Greenville, won the Nobel Prize in Physics for his efforts in laser development.

The Peachoid water tower is in Gaffney, home of the South Carolina Peach Festival.

COLUMBIA

In the 1830s Sarah and Angelina Grimké were among the first women to speak out publicly against slavery and for women's rights.

Early Charleston was a city of wealthy planters and merchants. Known for religious tolerance, it attracted French Protestants (Huguenots) and Jews.

State hospitality beverage: Tea

S.C. Tea

West African people, who began arriving in the Sea Islands as slaves some three hundred years ago, created a culture and language called Gullah, which still exists today.

Myrtle Beach, an oceanside resort, was named after the sweet myrtle tree.

Sumter

Myrtle Beach

Pawleys Island

Atlantic Ocean

North Charleston

Charleston

Fort Sumter National Monument

The Citadel, Charleston

State flower: Yellow jessamine

Legend has it that Drayton Hall plantation house was saved during the Civil War by John Drayton, a doctor, who posted quarantine signs outside.

Hilton Head Island

Sea Islands

IT HAPPENED HERE:
The first shots of the Civil War were fired on Fort Sumter in 1861.

State bird: Carolina wren

In 1744 Eliza Pinckney successfully grew indigo on her father's plantation and made much-desired blue dye from it. Indigo joined rice as a staple of the Carolina economy.

alex. the pawleys island rope hammock was invented by a riverboat captain looking for a cool way to sleep. ben

State tree: Palmetto

PRAISE HOUSE

Dear Grandma,
On Hilton Head Island we met a Gullah woman who makes sweetgrass baskets. She taught us some Gullah words.
Lub (that means "love"), Annie

SOUTH CAROLINA
1788
Drayton Hall

Otis Redding, soul music singer and songwriter (1941–1967)

Flannery O'Connor, acclaimed writer (1925–1964)

John Pemberton, inventor of Coca-Cola (1831–1888)

Carson McCullers, author, The Member of the Wedding (1917–1967)

Ralph McGill, publisher, known as "the Conscience of the South" (1898–1969)

Martin Luther King Jr., Nobel Peace Prize–winning civil rights leader (1929–1968)

"Georgia, Georgia, the whole day through, just an old sweet song keeps Georgia on my mind...

Words by Stuart Gorrell, music by Hoagy Carmichael

GEORGIA ★
1788

Civil War figures Jefferson Davis, Stonewall Jackson, and Robert E. Lee are carved into Stone Mountain.

Blue Ridge Mountains

• Dahlonega

ATLANTA ★ □ Stone Mountain

Martin Luther King Jr. preached at the Ebenezer Baptist Church in Atlanta.

The Atlanta Cyclorama depicts the Battle of Atlanta.

CYCLORAMA

• Columbus

Macon

Plains

Ashburn

Jimmy Carter, of Plains, was a peanut farmer before he became our thirty-ninth president. In 2002 he won the Nobel Peace Prize.

Okefenokee Swamp

The Waving Girl statue greets ships in Savannah's harbor.

Augusta

Vidalia onions

Vidalia.

Savannah

Golden Isles

Atlantic Ocean

Martin Luther King Jr., Nobel Peace Prize–winning civil rights leader (1929–1968)

Margaret Mitchell, author, Gone with the Wind (1900–1949)

Johnny Mercer, Academy Award–winning songwriter (1909–1976)

James Oglethorpe, founder of Georgia (1696–1785)

Bobby Jones, champion golfer (1902–1971)

State bird: Brown thrasher

After gold was discovered in the late 1820s, Dahlonega became a gold rush town.

According to legend, Cherokee roses grew along the Trail of Tears, which Cherokees walked when they were forced to move west.

State flower: Cherokee rose

alex. did you ever see a ten-foot-tall peanut? i did—in ashburn. ben

GEORGIA is in PEANUTS

Walt Kelly created Pogo after he visited Okefenokee Swamp in 1942.

Blind Willie McTell, blues guitar pioneer (c. 1901–1959)

Sidney Lanier, poet (1842–1881)

Ty Cobb, baseball star (1886–1961)

alex. i stood in the olympic park's fountain of rings and hardly got wet. ben

Centennial Olympic Park, Atlanta

Dear Grandma, People in Georgia love peaches and pecans—and put peanuts in their Coke! Love, Annie

Oliver Hardy, comic-film star (1892–1957)

Martha Berry, founder of Berry College (1866–1942)

Georgia, Georgia, no peace I find, just an old sweet song. the road leads back to you.

Other arms reach out to me, other eyes smile tenderly. Still in peaceful dreams I see keeps Georgia on my mind

Lewis Grizzard, author and humorist (1946–1994)

Jackie Robinson, baseball player, broke racial barrier in major leagues (1919–1972)

Juliette Gordon Low, founder of Girl Scouts of the U.S.A. (1860–1927)

Crawford Long, physician, first to use anesthesia in surgery (1815–1878)

Ma Rainey, singer, called "the Mother of the Blues" (1886–1939)

Ray Charles, beloved composer, pianist, and singer (1930–2004)

"Florida is...a riot of color in nature~glistening green leaves, pink, blue, purple, yellow

Seagulls

Banana tree

State flower: Orange blossom

Juan Ponce de León landed in Florida in 1513. Arriving around Easter, he named the new land Florida after Pascua Florida, the Spanish name for the holiday.

Making liquid-nitrogen ice cream at the National High Magnetic Field Laboratory, in Tallahassee

The navy's Blue Angel flight squadron trains near Pensacola's National Museum of Naval Aviation.

Pensacola   TALLAHASSEE

Florida Panther

When the U.S. government began to force Native Americans to move west in the 1830s, the Seminoles, under the leadership of brave warriors like Osceola, resisted. In the end many Seminoles had to move west, but some escaped into the Everglades, and their descendants remain in Florida today.

Florida was under Spanish control, then British, then Spanish again, before being conveyed to the United States in 1821.

★ FLORIDA ★
STATEHOOD 1845

Everglades

Sugarcane

State bird: Mockingbird

In the early decades of the nineteenth century, artist and naturalist John James Audubon traveled in Florida searching for exotic birds to draw.

Dear Grandpa,
If you came here in the winter and went home in the spring, you'd be a snowbird, which is what Floridians call all the retired people who do that.
From, Ben

"There are no other Everglades in the world. They are . . . one of the unique regions of the earth, remote, never wholly known. Nothing anywhere else is like them."
—Marjory Stoneman Douglas

Great blue heron

Reddish egret

Flamingo

American white pelican

Anhinga

Roseate Spoonbill

Alligator

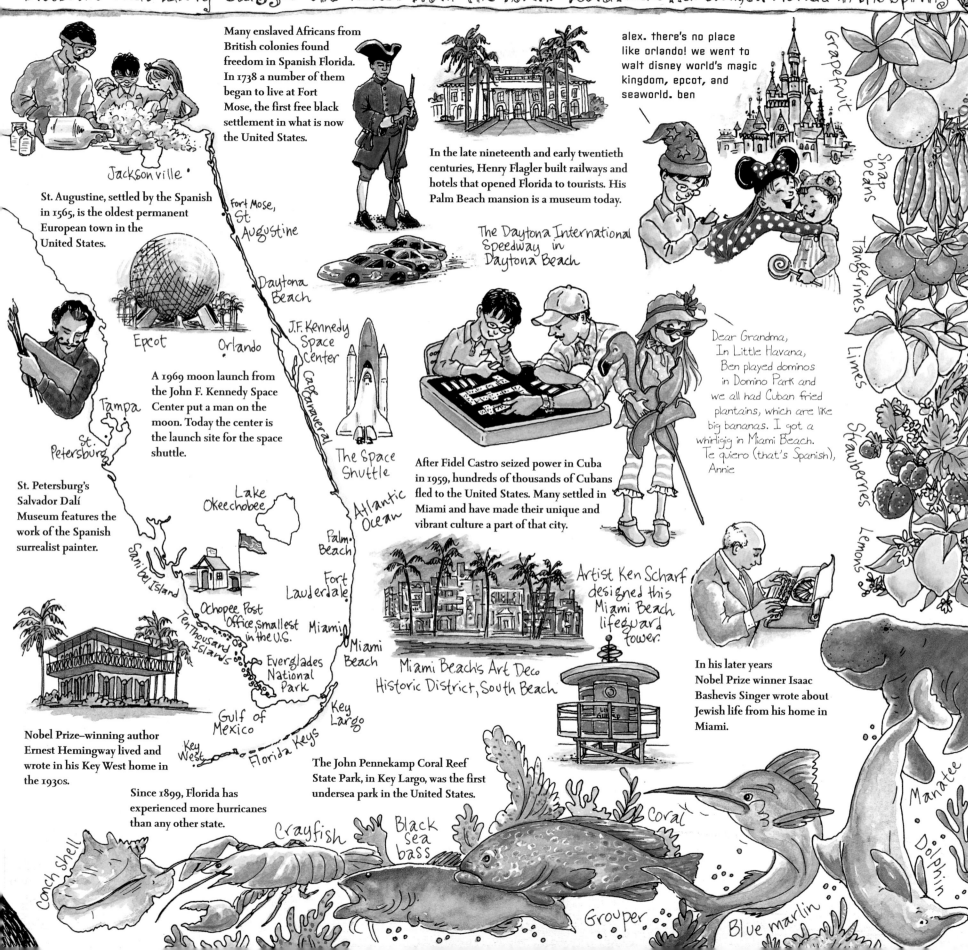

Many enslaved Africans from British colonies found freedom in Spanish Florida. In 1738 a number of them began to live at Fort Mose, the first free black settlement in what is now the United States.

alex. there's no place like orlando! we went to walt disney world's magic kingdom, epcot, and seaworld. ben

Jacksonville

St. Augustine, settled by the Spanish in 1565, is the oldest permanent European town in the United States.

Fort Mose, St. Augustine

In the late nineteenth and early twentieth centuries, Henry Flagler built railways and hotels that opened Florida to tourists. His Palm Beach mansion is a museum today.

The Daytona International Speedway in Daytona Beach

Daytona Beach

Epcot

Orlando

J.F. Kennedy Space Center

Cape Canaveral

A 1969 moon launch from the John F. Kennedy Space Center put a man on the moon. Today the center is the launch site for the space shuttle.

The Space Shuttle

Tampa

St. Petersburg

St. Petersburg's Salvador Dalí Museum features the work of the Spanish surrealist painter.

Lake Okeechobee

Atlantic Ocean

Dear Grandma,
In Little Havana, Ben played dominos in Domino Park and we all had Cuban fried plantains, which are like big bananas. I got a whirligig in Miami Beach.
Te quiero (that's Spanish), Annie

After Fidel Castro seized power in Cuba in 1959, hundreds of thousands of Cubans fled to the United States. Many settled in Miami and have made their unique and vibrant culture a part of that city.

Grapefruit

Snap beans

Tangerines

Limes

Strawberries

Lemons

Sanibel Island

Ten Thousand Islands

Ochopee Post Office, smallest in the U.S.

Palm Beach

Fort Lauderdale

Miami

Miami Beach

Everglades National Park

Gulf of Mexico

Key Largo

Key West

Florida Keys

Miami Beach's Art Deco Historic District, South Beach

Artist Ken Scharf designed this Miami Beach lifeguard tower.

In his later years Nobel Prize winner Isaac Bashevis Singer wrote about Jewish life from his home in Miami.

Nobel Prize–winning author Ernest Hemingway lived and wrote in his Key West home in the 1930s.

The John Pennekamp Coral Reef State Park, in Key Largo, was the first undersea park in the United States.

Since 1899, Florida has experienced more hurricanes than any other state.

Conch Shell

Crayfish

Black sea bass

Coral

Manatee

Grouper

Blue marlin

Dolphin

ALABAMIAN
SPORTS
LEGENDS

Joe Louis

Paul "Bear" Bryant

Willie Mays

Jesse Owens

Hank Aaron

alex. we went spelunking (that's cave exploring) in desoto caverns. the giant stalactites were awesome! ben

Alabama produces many crops, but cotton is the leading one.

State bird: Yellowhammer   State flower: Camellia

★ ALABAMA ★
STATEHOOD 1819

Tuscumbia

Huntsville

Tennessee River

Little River

Blind and deaf, Helen Keller, of Tuscumbia, learned her first word while water from this pump was flowing over her hand.

Appalachian Mountains

Football rivals: Auburn and the University of Alabama

War Eagle!

Roll Tide!

Rosa Parks's 1955 refusal to give up her seat on a Montgomery bus ushered in the modern civil rights movement.

Birmingham

DeSoto Caverns

IT HAPPENED HERE: In 1965 thousands of civil rights protesters marched from Selma to Montgomery.

Birmingham's fifty-six-foot-tall statue of the Roman god Vulcan shows the importance of iron mills to the building of that city.

"Space Shot", U.S. Space and Rocket Center, Huntsville

Tombigbee River

Selma

MONTGOMERY

Tuskegee

Civil Rights Memorial fountain, Montgomery

GEORGE WASHINGTON CARVER MUSEUM

Alabamian Harper Lee published only one book, the Pulitzer Prize–winning To Kill a Mockingbird.

"Until justice rolls down like waters and righteousness like a mighty stream." —Martin Luther King Jr.'s words inscribed on Montgomery's Civil Rights Memorial

The French, who were the first Europeans to settle in Alabama, began building Fort Condé in 1723. Today this replica fort is a place to learn about the history of Mobile.

Fort Condé Mobile

Musician, composer, and singer Nat "King" Cole, of Montgomery, is honored at the Alabama Jazz Hall of Fame in Birmingham.

Dear Grandma,
George Washington Carver figured out hundreds of things to make from peanuts—even glue and ink.
Love, Annie

I was waltz-ing with my dar-lin' to the Ten-nes-see Waltz when an old friend I hap-pened to see.

"Tennessee Waltz," by Redd Stewart and Pee Wee King, is one of Tennessee's five state songs.

State bird: Mockingbird

A replica of the Parthenon honors Nashville's reputation as "the Athens of the South."

TENNESSEE

Ruby Falls

STATEHOOD 1796

The Tennessee walking horse is known for its smooth gait.

Ruby Falls is a 145-foot waterfall inside a limestone cave within Lookout Mountain.

Near Limestone is a replica of the home of Davy Crockett: frontiersman, politician, and defender of the Alamo.

Elvis's pink Cadillac, Graceland, Memphis

Cadillac

Andrew Jackson
7th President

James K. Polk
11th President

Andrew Johnson
17th President

State flower: Iris

Reelfoot Lake

St. Bethlehem

NASHVILLE

Knoxville's Sunsphere, built for the 1982 World's Fair

Limestone

Reelfoot Lake was created by earthquakes in 1811 and 1812.

Mississippi River

Tennessee River

Knoxville

Pigeon Forge

Great Smoky Mountains

The world's longest-running live radio show, the Grand Ole Opry broadcasts from Nashville.

GRAND OLE OPRY

Tennessee River

Shiloh National Military Park

Memphis

Chattanooga

Lookout Mountain

Dear Grandma,
In Memphis we saw the Peabody hotel ducks' red carpet parade. Then we had yummy hickory-smoked barbecue!
Love,
Annie

After a childhood battle with polio, Wilma Rudolph, of St. Bethlehem, won Olympic gold medals in track and field.

alex. we went on the daredevil falls ride at dollywood in pigeon forge. ben

HOTEL
KING

Located at the site where Martin Luther King Jr. was killed, this Memphis museum explores his legacy.

In the early 1800s Sequoya invented an alphabet for the Cherokee language.

Yes, I lost my lit-tle dar-lin' the night they were play-ing the beau-ti-ful Ten-nes-see Waltz.

I re-mem-ber the night and the Ten-nes-see Waltz. Now I know just how much I have lost.

In-tro-duced him to my loved one and while they were waltz-ing my friend stole my sweet-heart from me.

"The sun shines bright in My Old Kentucky Home..."

Central Kentucky has the world's largest concentration of Thoroughbred breeding farms.

The National Corvette Museum is in Bowling Green, where Corvettes are produced.

Kentucky was the first state west of the Appalachian Mountains.

Kentucky Derby Museum

State bird: cardinal

Daniel Boone blazed the Wilderness Road through the Cumberland Gap to Kentucky in 1775. The route became an avenue for westward migration.

Daniel Boone

Dear Grandma,
The Kentucky Derby has been held every year since 1875. In the museum here at Churchill Downs, you can see what fancy hats people wear.
Love, Annie

Churchill Downs, Louisville

Ohio River

KENTUCKY
★ ★
STATEHOOD 1792

Louisville FRANKFORT
Lexington

Fort Knox

Abraham Lincoln Birthplace, Hodgenville

Daniel Boone National Forest

Home of bluegrass music

Kentucky got its nickname, the Bluegrass State, from a grass that produces blue purple buds in the spring.

State flower: Goldenrod

Owensboro

Jefferson Davis birthplace, Fairview

Land Between the Lakes

Mammoth Cave

Bowling Green

Mammoth Cave, with more than 360 underground miles mapped, is the longest recorded cave system in the world.

Corbin

Cumberland Gap

Appalachian Mountains

Billions of dollars of gold are kept inside the U.S. Bullion Depository at Fort Knox.

"Float like a butterfly, sting like a bee," said boxing great Muhammad Ali, born in Louisville.

Ashland, in the city of Lexington, was the home of Henry Clay, a statesman in the era before the Civil War.

In the 1930s Harland Sanders developed his special recipe for Kentucky Fried Chicken in Corbin.

At the Kentucky Vietnam Veterans Memorial, in Frankfort, a giant sundial's shadow touches the name of each veteran on the date of the person's death.

Dear Grandpa,
At the Louisville Slugger Museum we learned about all the great hitters who have used Louisville Slugger bats. And we saw the world's biggest bat. It's a replica of one Babe Ruth used.
From, Ben

"Happy birthday, dear Ben..." "Happy birthday to you!"

The tune for "Happy Birthday to You" was copyrighted in 1893 by Louisville sisters Mildred and Patty Hill.

Both U.S. president Abraham Lincoln and Confederate president Jefferson Davis were born in log cabins in Kentucky, less than a year and about a hundred miles apart.

Tecumseh 1768–1813 — Shawnee leader

The Toledo Zoo, famous for its Hippoquarium

William Henry Harrison 1773–1841 — 9th President

The National First Ladies' Library, in Canton

Ulysses S. Grant 1822–1885 — 18th President

The birthplace of inventor Thomas Edison, in Milan

Rutherford B. Hayes 1822–1893 — 19th President

Severance Hall, home of the world-class Cleveland Orchestra

James Thurber 1894–1961 — Writer/humorist

Butterflies in Columbus's Franklin Park Conservatory

Paul Laurence Dunbar 1872–1906 — Poet

The Pro Football Hall of Fame, in Canton

Annie Oakley 1860–1926 — Sharpshooter

The world's largest Amish community, centered in Wayne, Holmes, and Tuscarawas counties

Warren Harding 1865–1923 — 29th president

Finney Chapel, at Oberlin College, the first college to admit women in the United States

William H. Taft 1857–1930 — 27th president

The Dayton bike shop of aviation pioneers Wilbur and Orville Wright

William McKinley 1843–1901 — 25th president

Ohio's state song describes natural beauty, grand cities, and mighty industry. "Beautiful Ohio, thy wonders are in view, land where all my dreams come true!"

Ohio's farms produce many foods, including soybeans, tomatoes, and corn.

OHIO STATEHOOD 1803

State bird: Cardinal

The Tyler Davidson Fountain, in Cincinnati

James Garfield 1831–1881 — 20th President

The Contemporary Arts Center, designed by Zaha Hadid, in Cincinnati

Benjamin Harrison 1833–1901 — 23rd President

The Cincinnati Red Stockings, the first professional baseball team, 1869

Dear Grandma,
In Cleveland, Dad and Mom got a big kick out of the Rock & Roll Hall of Fame, where we saw stuff like John Lennon's report card.
Love, Annie

Johnny Appleseed planted trees in at least fifteen Ohio counties.

William McGuffey's schoolbooks, first published in Cincinnati in 1836, helped teach moral values to millions of American children.

Around a thousand years old and more than a thousand feet long, the Serpent Mound was built by prehistoric people.

Toledo · Lake Erie · Cleveland · Oberlin · Milan · Akron · Wapakoneta · Canton · COLUMBUS · Marietta · Cincinnati · Serpent Mound · Ohio River · Hocking Hills State Park

Since 1936 — All-American Soap Box Derby, Akron

State flower: Red carnation

alex. amazing! 24 astronauts came from ohio, including neil armstrong and john glenn. ben

The W. P. Snyder Jr., a steam-powered, stern-wheeled towboat, is the last of its kind in the United States.

Armstrong Air & Space Museum, Wapakoneta

Larry Bird, the Indiana Pacers

Knute Rockne, University of Notre Dame

Bob Knight, Indiana University

RENOWNED HOOSIER COACHES

alex. "hoosier hysteria" is what happens here during high school basketball season. ben

In the early 1800s, Shawnee leader Tecumseh united Indian nations to protect Indian lands. In 1811 his warriors fought with troops led by future president William Henry Harrison near Tippecanoe Creek.

Indiana, known as the Crossroads of America, has some twelve thousand miles of state and interstate highways running through it.

★ INDIANA ★
1848 BRIDGETON
Bridgeton Covered Bridge
STATEHOOD 1816

Lake Michigan

Gary

South Bend

University of Notre Dame

State bird: Cardinal

Fort Wayne

Madame C. J. Walker, born in 1867 to former slaves, became one of the first female millionaires by developing and selling hair-care products for African Americans.

Tippecanoe Battlefield

Kokomo

West Lafayette

IT HAPPENED HERE: On July 4, 1894, in Kokomo, inventor Elwood Haynes successfully tested a gasoline-powered car.

The Indianapolis Motor Speedway, which opened in 1909, is home of the Indianapolis (Indy) 500 race, held annually at the end of May.

The rebuilding of the Bridgeton Bridge brought the total of covered bridges in Indiana to ninety-one.

Like his grandfather William Henry Harrison, Benjamin Harrison became president of the United States.

Benjamin Harrison (1833-1901) 23rd president

Purdue University, in West Lafayette, is called "the Cradle of Astronauts." Twenty-two have been educated here.

Engineering Fountain at Purdue University

Hagerstown

INDIANAPOLIS

Bridgeton

Abraham Lincoln grew up in Indiana.

Bloomington

Indiana University

Since 1890, Abbott's Candy has been an Indiana family business in Hagerstown.

The 285-foot Soldiers and Sailors Monument in Indianapolis is one of many Indiana monuments honoring those who served.

Lincoln Boyhood National Memorial

Evansville

Ohio River

Who's there? Whose ear?

Dear Grandma, People in Indiana call themselves "Hoosiers"—so far I've heard seven different reasons why! Love, Annie

Indiana native Orville Redenbacher helped the state become one of the largest popcorn producers in the nation.

Hoosier poet James Whitcomb Riley, of Indianapolis, is best known for "Little Orphant Annie," first published in 1885.

State flower: Peony

Indianapolis Motor Speedway Hall of Fame Museum

Ransom Olds started the Olds Motor Vehicle Company in Lansing, Michigan, in 1897. Within a decade David Buick and Henry Ford also started car companies, and Ford went on to develop the assembly line, a basis of much industrial production. By 1925, General Motors, Chevrolet, and Chrysler were also producing cars, and Detroit was being called Motor City.

Ransom E. Olds and the 1st "Olds"
☆ 1896 ☆

In 1668 Father Jacques Marquette, a Jesuit missionary living among the Great Lakes Indians, founded Michigan's first permanent settlement at Sault Sainte Marie.

MICHIGAN
STATEHOOD 1837

During the nineteenth century Michigan led the nation in lumber production, supplying the white pine that built cities and railroads.

1st Buick, built by Walter L. Marr
☆ ca. 1899 ☆

State bird: Robin

The name Michigan comes from two Native American words: michi, meaning "large," and gama, meaning "lake."

The Keweenaw National Historical Park preserves the area's copper-mining heritage.

Lake Superior

Keweenaw National Historical Park

Marquette

Upper Peninsula

Sault Sainte Marie

Mackinac Island

In 1895 J. W. Westcott started a marine mail service. Today this tugboat named after him delivers to vessels on the Great Lakes.

State Stone: Petoskey

Dear Grandma,
We rode in carriages on Mackinac Island—because no cars are allowed!
Love, Annie

Mackinac Island

Founded in 1928, Interlochen Center for the Arts is today one of America's foremost academies for training talented youth.

Interlochen

Lake Michigan

Thirty-eighth president Gerald R. Ford grew up in Grand Rapids.

• Grand Rapids
• Holland

LANSING

Warren

Detroit

Lake St. Clair

Lower Peninsula

Lake Huron

Lake Ontario

Lake Erie

State flower: Apple blossom

In the 1760s Pontiac, an Ottawa leader, organized resistance against British rule.

The Bowl at Interlochen

Cadillac's step-in closed-car design
☆ 1905 ☆

Six million tulips bloom in the city of Holland each May.

Motown Records, founded in Detroit by Berry Gordy in 1959, gave Stevie Wonder, Diana Ross, and many other African-American musicians their start.

alex. they have cherry pit spitting contests in michigan. champions can shoot a pit more than 90 feet! ben

The Oscar Mayer Wienermobile at the Henry Ford Museum

The Henry Ford Museum, near Detroit, honors American innovators.

Henry Ford and the Model A
☆ 1903 ☆

From 1885 to 1925 political leader Robert La Follette fought for reforms.

The Experimental Aircraft Association's museum, in Oshkosh, hosts the international Fly-in Convention.

German, Polish, Irish, Norwegian, and other European immigrants came to Wisconsin in the nineteenth century, bringing many skills, including dairy farming, to the state.

The Milwaukee Art Museum has a pavilion, designed by Santiago Calatrava, with wings that open and close.

Margarethe Schurz opened America's first kindergarten in Watertown in 1856.

The International Clown Hall of Fame, outside Milwaukee, is dedicated to the art and history of clowning.

On a Sunday in 1881, Two Rivers druggist Edward Berner served syrup over ice cream, creating a "sundae."

The Menominees, Ojibwas, and Potawatomis were among the original inhabitants of Wisconsin.

In 1885 Bernard Cigrand, of Waubeka, commemorated Flag Day and started a tradition.

Golda Meir, Israeli prime minister from 1969 to 1974, grew up in Milwaukee.

Born in Ripon in 1859, Carrie Chapman Catt became a leader in the suffrage movement.

Renowned magician Harry Houdini is celebrated at the Outagamie Museum in his hometown of Appleton.

There are more than a hundred figures sculpted by former lumberjack Fred Smith at Wisconsin Concrete Park, in Phillips.

Baraboo's Circus World Museum preserves original Ringling Bros. wagons and other circus artifacts.

Part of the National Fresh Water Fishing Hall of Fame and Museum, in Hayward, is housed inside a replica of a muskie.

In 1903 the first Harley-Davidson motorcycle was created by William Harley and Arthur Davidson in Milwaukee.

Burger Fest in Seymour commemorates fifteen-year-old Charlie Nagreen's 1885 creation of the hamburger.

Architect and Wisconsinite Frank Lloyd Wright, born in 1867, designed and lived in Taliesin, in Spring Green.

WISCONSIN ★ STATEHOOD 1848 ★

American Birkebeiner, Hayward

State bird: Robin

State flower: Wood Violet

GO PACKERS 4

Lake Superior
Apostle Islands
Hayward
Phillips
Mississippi River
Seymour
Appleton
Green Bay
Oshkosh
Two Rivers
Ripon
Green Bay
Door Peninsula
Lake Michigan
Wisconsin Dells
Waubeka
Baraboo
MADISON
Watertown
Spring Green
New Glarus
Milwaukee
Racine

Floodwaters created the dramatic rock formations of Wisconsin Dells about fifteen thousand years ago.

Dear Grandma, Wisconsinites produce over two billion pounds of cheese each year. I guess that's why they call themselves "Cheeseheads"! Love, Annie

alex. at the winter festival in new glarus they blow alpenhorns to call in on early spring. ben

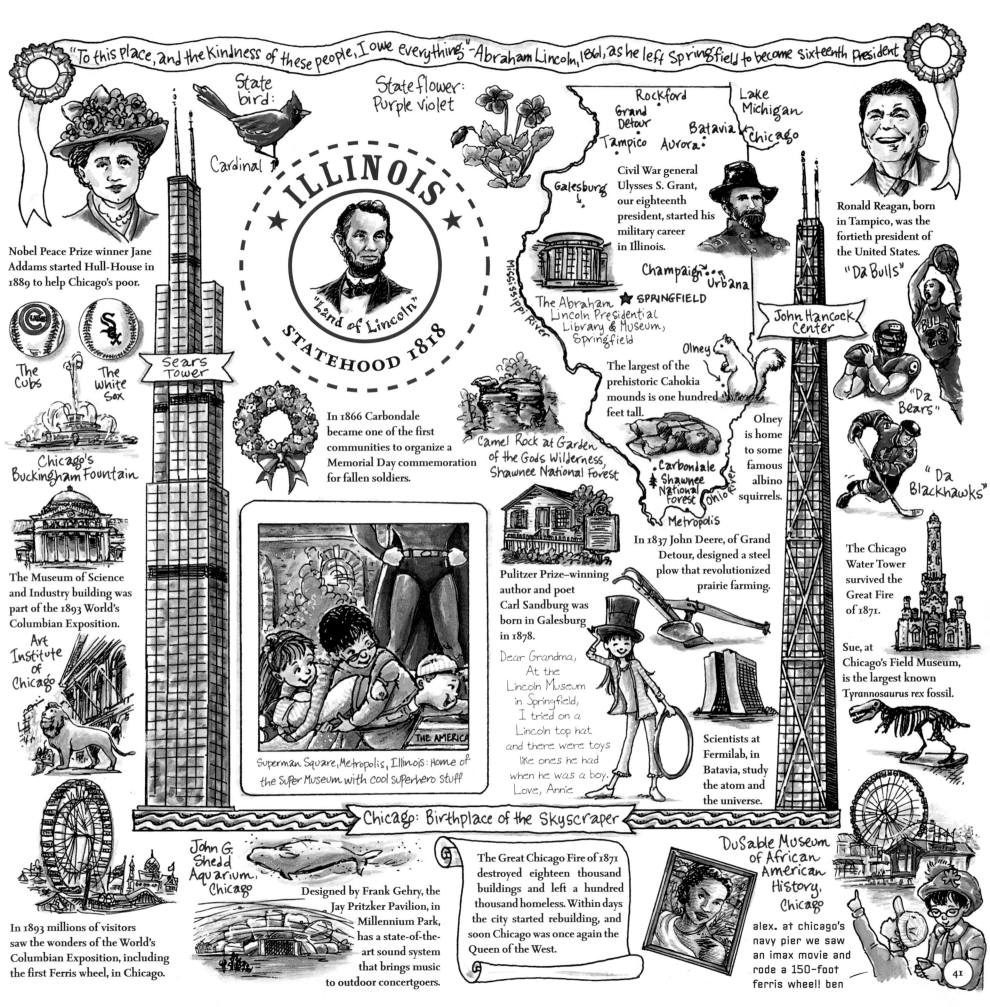

"To this place, and the kindness of these people, I owe everything." —Abraham Lincoln, 1861, as he left Springfield to become sixteenth president

State bird: Cardinal

State flower: Purple violet

ILLINOIS
"Land of Lincoln"
STATEHOOD 1818

Rockford
Grand Detour
Tampico
Aurora
Batavia
Lake Michigan
Chicago
Galesburg
Mississippi River

Nobel Peace Prize winner Jane Addams started Hull-House in 1889 to help Chicago's poor.

The Cubs

The White Sox

Chicago's Buckingham Fountain

The Museum of Science and Industry building was part of the 1893 World's Columbian Exposition.

Art Institute of Chicago

Sears Tower

In 1866 Carbondale became one of the first communities to organize a Memorial Day commemoration for fallen soldiers.

Camel Rock at Garden of the Gods Wilderness, Shawnee National Forest

Civil War general Ulysses S. Grant, our eighteenth president, started his military career in Illinois.

Champaign
Urbana

The Abraham Lincoln Presidential Library & Museum, Springfield

★ SPRINGFIELD

Olney

The largest of the prehistoric Cahokia mounds is one hundred feet tall.

Olney is home to some famous albino squirrels.

Carbondale
Shawnee National Forest
Ohio River
Metropolis

In 1837 John Deere, of Grand Detour, designed a steel plow that revolutionized prairie farming.

Ronald Reagan, born in Tampico, was the fortieth president of the United States.

"Da Bulls"

BULLS 23

"Da Bears"

"Da Blackhawks"

John Hancock Center

The Chicago Water Tower survived the Great Fire of 1871.

Sue, at Chicago's Field Museum, is the largest known Tyrannosaurus rex fossil.

Superman Square, Metropolis, Illinois: Home of the Super Museum with cool superhero stuff

THE AMERICA

Pulitzer Prize–winning author and poet Carl Sandburg was born in Galesburg in 1878.

Dear Grandma,
At the Lincoln Museum in Springfield, I tried on a Lincoln top hat and there were toys like ones he had when he was a boy.
Love, Annie

Scientists at Fermilab, in Batavia, study the atom and the universe.

Chicago: Birthplace of the Skyscraper

John G. Shedd Aquarium, Chicago

In 1893 millions of visitors saw the wonders of the World's Columbian Exposition, including the first Ferris wheel, in Chicago.

Designed by Frank Gehry, the Jay Pritzker Pavilion, in Millennium Park, has a state-of-the-art sound system that brings music to outdoor concertgoers.

The Great Chicago Fire of 1871 destroyed eighteen thousand buildings and left a hundred thousand homeless. Within days the city started rebuilding, and soon Chicago was once again the Queen of the West.

DuSable Museum of African American History, Chicago

alex. at chicago's navy pier we saw an imax movie and rode a 150-foot ferris wheel! ben

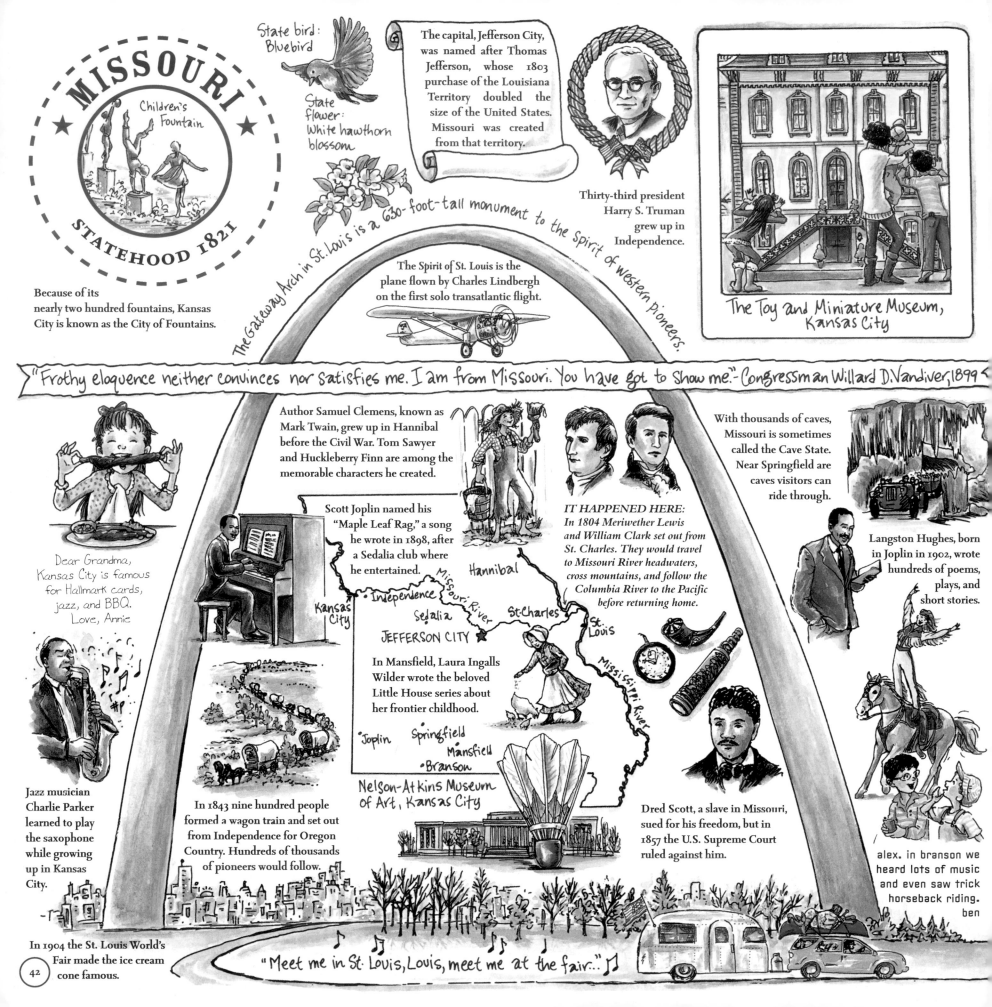

MISSOURI
Children's Fountain
STATEHOOD 1821

State bird: Bluebird

State flower: White hawthorn blossom

The capital, Jefferson City, was named after Thomas Jefferson, whose 1803 purchase of the Louisiana Territory doubled the size of the United States. Missouri was created from that territory.

Thirty-third president Harry S. Truman grew up in Independence.

The Toy and Miniature Museum, Kansas City

Because of its nearly two hundred fountains, Kansas City is known as the City of Fountains.

The Gateway Arch in St. Louis is a 630-foot-tall monument to the spirit of western pioneers.

The Spirit of St. Louis is the plane flown by Charles Lindbergh on the first solo transatlantic flight.

"Frothy eloquence neither convinces nor satisfies me. I am from Missouri. You have got to show me." —Congressman Willard D. Vandiver, 1899

Author Samuel Clemens, known as Mark Twain, grew up in Hannibal before the Civil War. Tom Sawyer and Huckleberry Finn are among the memorable characters he created.

With thousands of caves, Missouri is sometimes called the Cave State. Near Springfield are caves visitors can ride through.

Dear Grandma, Kansas City is famous for Hallmark cards, jazz, and BBQ. Love, Annie

Scott Joplin named his "Maple Leaf Rag," a song he wrote in 1898, after a Sedalia club where he entertained.

IT HAPPENED HERE: In 1804 Meriwether Lewis and William Clark set out from St. Charles. They would travel to Missouri River headwaters, cross mountains, and follow the Columbia River to the Pacific before returning home.

Langston Hughes, born in Joplin in 1902, wrote hundreds of poems, plays, and short stories.

In Mansfield, Laura Ingalls Wilder wrote the beloved Little House series about her frontier childhood.

Hannibal
Missouri River
Independence
Sedalia
St. Charles
Kansas City
JEFFERSON CITY
St. Louis
Mississippi River
Joplin
Springfield
Mansfield
Branson

Nelson-Atkins Museum of Art, Kansas City

Jazz musician Charlie Parker learned to play the saxophone while growing up in Kansas City.

In 1843 nine hundred people formed a wagon train and set out from Independence for Oregon Country. Hundreds of thousands of pioneers would follow.

Dred Scott, a slave in Missouri, sued for his freedom, but in 1857 the U.S. Supreme Court ruled against him.

alex. in branson we heard lots of music and even saw trick horseback riding. ben

In 1904 the St. Louis World's Fair made the ice cream cone famous.

"Meet me in St. Louis, Louis, meet me at the fair..."

"I believe in Arkansas as a land of opportunity and promise." ~The Arkansas Creed, 1972

State flower: Apple blossom

State bird: Mockingbird

On the third Monday of February, Arkansans honor Daisy Gatson Bates, whose efforts led to the desegregation of Little Rock's Central High School in 1957.

Dear Grandpa,
The Ozarks are so beautiful. They're filled with what some old-timers used to call "hollers" and "knobs." (That's valleys and hills.)
From,
Ben

Pea Ridge National Military Park

• Rogers

Fayetteville

Buffalo River

Alma

• Fort Smith

Mountain View

The Ozark Folk Center, north of Mountain View, preserves the music, dance, and craftsmanship of the Ozark region.

IT HAPPENED HERE:
In Little Rock in 1957, nine African-American students walked through the doors of Central High School and made civil rights history.

Old State House Museum, Little Rock

The historic town of Helena celebrates the Arkansas Blues and Heritage Festival every October.

Arkansas is a top producer of rice and broiler chickens.

Born in Hope, Bill Clinton became the forty-second president. His presidential library is in Little Rock.

★ LITTLE ROCK

• Hot Springs

Helena

MISSISSIPPI River

The MacArthur Museum of Arkansas Military History is named for war hero Gen. Douglas MacArthur, who was born in Little Rock.

• Pine Bluff

Crater of Diamonds State Park

Kingsland

Country music legend Johnny Cash was born in Kingsland.

Washington

Hope

Texarkana

The adjoining cities of Texarkana, Arkansas, and Texarkana, Texas, share a post office, which sits on the state line.

TEXARKANA STATE LINE
TEXAS ARKANSAS

The Jonquil Festival in Old Washington Historic State Park celebrates the coming of spring to southwest Arkansas.

ARKANSAS
★ ★
Buffalo National River
STATEHOOD 1836

The giant Wal-Mart chain got its start when Sam Walton opened a store in Rogers in 1962.

Arkansas is the only state that has passed a resolution on how to say its name. In 1881 the legislature declared the correct way is "AR-kan-SAW."

OZARK

Crater of Diamonds State Park

Dear Grandma,
At Crater of Diamonds State Park, you can dig for diamonds and keep what you find. Once somebody found a forty-carat diamond. Wish me luck!
Love, Annie

In 1932 Hattie Caraway became the first woman elected to the U.S. Senate.

For more than two hundred years, people have bathed in the hot springs flowing from Hot Springs Mountain. Historic bathhouses line Bathhouse Row in Hot Springs National Park.

Alma, Ark
SPINACH CAPITAL of the WORLD

Mississippi has produced many outstanding writers, including Eudora Welty, Tennessee Williams, and Richard Wright. "I discovered," wrote William Faulkner, perhaps the greatest Mississippi author, "that my own little postage stamp of native soil was worth writing about and that I would never live long enough to exhaust it."

State flower: Magnolia

When Faulkner, who lived in Oxford, accepted the Nobel Prize in 1950, he said that it was a writer's privilege to help people endure by lifting their hearts.

John Lee Hooker

Muddy Waters

B.B. King

The blues style probably originated in the Mississippi Delta, where many great blues artists were born.

State bird: Mockingbird

Every four years dancers from all over the world come to Jackson to compete in the USA International Ballet Competition.

MISSISSIPPI

Southern magnolia

STATEHOOD 1817

Teddy bears were first made by Rose Michtom in 1902, after President Teddy Roosevelt refused to shoot a bear in the Mississippi woods.

The Jim Henson Museum, in Leland, honors Henson's many creations, including Kermit the Frog.

Oxford

Leland

Belzoni

Dear Grandma,
They call Belzoni the Catfish Capital of the World, so we had fried catfish—and Mississippi mud pie for dessert!
Love, Annie

Before he was killed in 1963, Medgar Evers worked tirelessly to expand civil rights for African Americans.

Mississippi River

Vicksburg National Military Park commemorates the 47-day siege of Vicksburg, which occurred during the Civil War.

Vicksburg

JACKSON

Although Jackson was occupied four times during the Civil War and parts of the city burned, the Old Capitol, which today houses a museum, was spared.

Columbia

Natchez

"The Mad Potter of Biloxi," George Ohr, was a turn-of-the-century innovator of abstract pottery.

Mississippi native Leontyne Price became an international opera star.

In 1870 Hiram Revels, of Natchez, became the first African American to serve in the U.S. Senate.

Stanton Hall, Natchez

In the springtime in Natchez, as many as thirty mansions from before the Civil War are open for tours.

Pascagoula
Gulfport
Biloxi
Long Beach

The ancient Friendship Oak, in Long Beach, has survived Hurricanes Camille and Katrina. Its endurance symbolizes the strength of Gulf Coast residents who are building again.

alex. the pascagoula river is sometimes called the singing river because of the humming sound it makes. ben

AMERICAN QUEEN

A river road for generations of explorers and settlers, the mighty Mississippi has long given Americans a sense of great distances and possibilities.

LOUISIANA
★ STATEHOOD 1812 ★

Bayou Teche

The Spanish moss draping the cypresses and live oaks along the banks of Louisiana's bayous is related to the pineapple.

State bird: Brown pelican

Jimmie Davis cowrote one of Louisiana's state songs, "You Are My Sunshine," before he became governor.

Festival International de Louisiane, Lafayette

Dear Grandma,
In Lafayette we went to a "fais do-do" (a dance party) where they had a zydeco band. The musicians played an accordion, a guitar, and a rubboard (a washboard).
Adieu, Annie

Both gospel singer Mahalia Jackson and jazz great Louis Armstrong were born in New Orleans.

State flower: Magnolia

Cotton and sugarcane were mainstays of the plantation economy.

Shreveport

The Chapel at American Rose Center

The American Rose Center, near Shreveport, showcases America's national floral emblem.

Descendants of early Louisianans from France, Spain, and Africa helped create Creole culture. French-speaking people driven from Canada and known as Acadians were the original Cajuns.

In 1987 eighteen white alligators were found in a nest near Houma.

The state capitol building, the idea of Governor Huey Long, was finished in 1932 and is the nation's tallest.

Mississippi River

After teaching at Louisiana State University, Robert Penn Warren wrote All the King's Men, a fictional version of Huey Long's life.

IT HAPPENED HERE: In New Orleans at the turn of the twentieth century, black musicians played a new kind of music, jazz, an original American art form.

Mardi Gras has been celebrated in New Orleans for more than two hundred years. In 2006 the parades, balls, and dancing signaled the determination of New Orleanians and Louisianans to preserve their heritage and overcome the devastation of Hurricane Katrina.

alex. cajun food uses lots of local plants and animals, and that includes alligators, crawfish, and turtles! ben

McIlhenny Tabasco sauce has been made in Avery Island from a secret family recipe since 1868.

FROG XING RAYNE, LA

Rayne is known as the Frog Capital of the World.

Rayne • Lafayette
• St. Martinville
Avery Island
★ BATON ROUGE
Lake Pontchartrain
New Orleans
Lafitte •
Bayou Teche   Houma
Gulf of Mexico

PRESERVATION HALL JAZZ BAND New Orleans, La.

A museum at the Longfellow-Evangeline State Historic Site, in St. Martinville, tells the story of the Acadian exile from Canada in 1755.

Dear Grandpa,
The famous pirate Jean Lafitte helped the Americans fighting under Andrew Jackson defeat the British at the Battle of New Orleans in 1815.
From, Ben

45

In the 1820s Stephen Austin, called the "Father of Texas," established the first Anglo-American colony along the Brazos River. Three hundred families joined him there.

Jim Bowie and Davy Crockett, fierce fighters both, were killed at the Battle of the Alamo in 1836.

Morning glory

Sam Houston led Texans to victory at the Battle of San Jacinto in 1836, then became president of the Republic of Texas.

Texas star

Free blacks and enslaved people accompanied early Spanish explorers to Texas. Juneteenth celebrates June 19, 1865, when news arrived that slavery had ended.

Texas thistle

Texas Paintbrush

The Lady Bird Johnson Wildflower Center, in Austin, was founded by the former First Lady to educate people about native plants.

Sunflower

Babe Didrikson Zaharias, of Port Arthur, has been called the greatest woman athlete of the early twentieth century.

Fiesta San Antonio

Fiesta San Antonio celebrates the multicultural heritage of Texas.

The Lone Star flag, adopted by the Republic of Texas in 1839, became the flag of the Lone Star State when Texas became part of the United States in 1845.

"The stars at night are big and bright,

Texas is bigger than most countries in Europe.

alex. it seems that everything in texas is really big. big bend national park, where we're headed next, covers more than 800,000 acres. ben

Forty-foot-tall boot, North Star Mall, San Antonio

El Paso

The Spanish names of cities like El Paso, "the Pass," reflect the history of Texas.

The Rio Grande Serres

Rio Grande

Dear Grandma,
We stopped at the Lighthouse, a rock formation in Palo Duro Canyon State Park, then had a cowboy breakfast of eggs, sausage, and biscuits slathered with brown gravy.
Yippee-Ki-Yi-yea!
Love, Annie

Three presidents have been elected from Texas: Lyndon B. Johnson, George H. W. Bush, and George W. Bush.

TEXAS
★ ★
Big Bend National Park
Castolon Historic District
STATEHOOD 1845

alex. the texas horned lizard defends itself by shooting blood from its eyes. cool! ben

The Sixth Floor Museum, located at the site in Dallas from which President John F. Kennedy was assassinated, explores his life, death, and legacy.

The famous oil gusher at Spindletop shot a hundred feet into the air when it was first tapped in 1901, setting off an oil boom.

Exhibits at the Petroleum Museum, in Midland, go back millions of years to show how oil was created.

Beavertail cactus

Mexican hat

Spiderwort

The Devil's Rope Museum, in McLean, tells the story of how the nineteenth-century invention of barbed wire transformed the West.

Chocolate flower

In 1900 a hurricane destroyed Galveston in the worst natural disaster in American history. Citizens rebuilt then, just as they have more recently in Beaumont and Port Arthur.

Prickly poppy

More than thirty ranch structures have been relocated to the National Ranching Heritage Center, in Lubbock.

Buffalo bur

The geodesic dome atop Reunion Tower is part of the world-famous Dallas skyline.

Texas vervain

deep in the heart of Texas; the prairie sky is wide and high, deep in the heart of Texas." —Hershey/Swander, circa 1941

Amarillo
McLean
Palo Duro Canyon

Texas produces more cotton than any other state.

Lubbock

Midland
Odessa

IT HAPPENED HERE: *In 1836 in San Antonio, 189 defenders of the Alamo held off the Mexican army for thirteen days before being overrun. "Remember the Alamo!" became a rallying cry for Texans.*

Fort Worth

Waco

Dallas

San Jacinto
★ AUSTIN
San Antonio
Houston
Beaumont
Galveston
Port Arthur

The Amon Carter Museum, in Fort Worth, houses art of the American West.

Waco's Texas Ranger Hall of Fame and Museum traces the story of these legendary lawmen.

Pioneer Plaza in Dallas has bronze statues of three cowboys driving a herd of forty longhorn steers.

From March to November up to a million and a half Mexican free-tailed bats make nightly flights from Austin's Congress Avenue Bridge.

The National Cowgirl Museum and Hall of Fame, in Fort Worth, honors the pioneer women of the American West.

Indian blanket

Big Bend National Park

San Antonio Missions National Historical Park preserves four missions from the late seventeenth and early eighteenth centuries.

as the International boundary between the U.S. and Mexico.

Mission San Jose, San Antonio

King Ranch

Padre Island

Corpus Christi

King Ranch, known as the birthplace of American ranching, is larger in size than Rhode Island.

The USS Lexington, in Corpus Christi, is the nation's longest-serving aircraft carrier.

Mockingbird: State bird

The San Jacinto Monument, 570 feet tall, honors the heroes who fought for Texas's independence.

The main engine of a space shuttle can be seen at the Johnson Space Center, in Houston.

Ma Ferguson became the first female governor of Texas in 1925.

In 1958, at the height of the Cold War, Van Cliburn, of Kilgore, won the International Tchaikovsky Competition in Moscow.

Purple prairie clover

Statue of rock 'n' roll legend Buddy Holly in his hometown, Lubbock

Padre Island National Seashore, the world's longest undeveloped stretch of barrier island, is a spot favored by bird-watchers. Thousands of species can be seen there.

Tickseed

In downtown Houston miles of air-conditioned pedestrian tunnels link hotels, offices, shops, and restaurants.

State flower: Bluebonnet

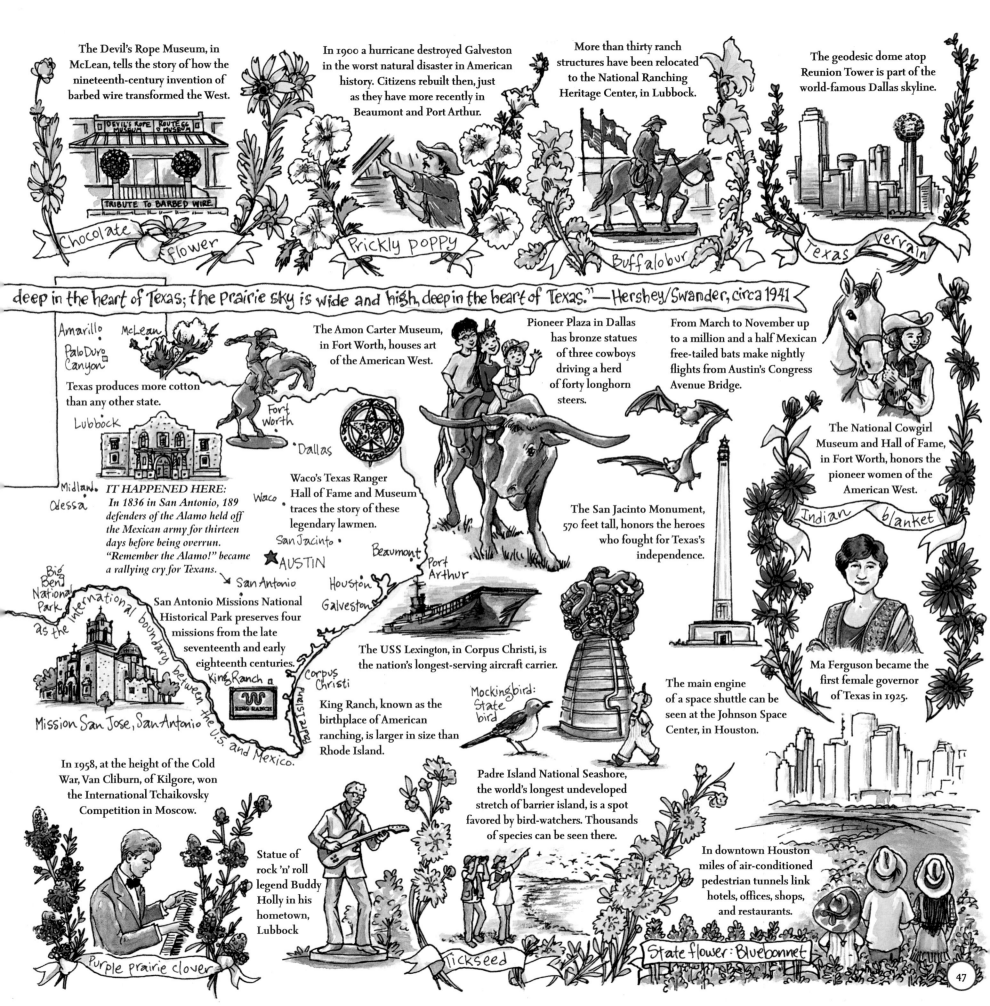

47

"We know we belong to the land, and the land we belong to is grand. And when we say: Ee-ee-ow! A-yip-i-o-ee-ay! We're only sayin', You're doin' fine, Oklahoma! Oklahoma, O.K.!"—From the official state song, "Oklahoma!" by Richard Rodgers and Oscar Hammerstein

Rich oil fields have drawn people to Oklahoma for more than a century. In 1935 the state legislature voted to authorize drilling around the state capitol in Oklahoma City.

State flower: Mistletoe

State bird: Scissor-tailed flycatcher

OKLAHOMA
State Capitol
STATEHOOD 1907

Chisholm Trail Heritage Center, Duncan

Dear Grandma, We had us some chicken-fried steak, and now Josh and Ben are fixin' to wrassle some critters! (That's cowboy talk—it's really me, Annie.) Love, Annie

Discoveryland!—in Tulsa—is the national home of Rodgers and Hammerstein's Oklahoma!

The End of the Trail statue, in Oklahoma City's National Cowboy and Western Heritage Museum

From 1867 to 1884 cowboys drove long-horned cattle from Texas across Oklahoma to Kansas along the Chisholm Trail.

CHISHOLM TRAIL

The Will Rogers Memorial Museum, in Claremore, displays the story of the beloved cowboy, humorist, and philosopher.

Cherokee National Capitol Building

The Pioneer Woman Museum is in Ponca City.

Commerce

The Cherokee Nation's capital, at Tahlequah, is at the end of the Trail of Tears, along which many Cherokees were forced to march in 1838–39.

The Sacred Rain Arrow statue at Gilcrease Museum, in Tulsa

• Beaver

alex. we went to the world championship cow chip throw in beaver. the record is over 185 feet! ben

The Oklahoma City National Memorial honors those who were killed and all whose lives were touched by the 1995 bombing of the Alfred P. Murrah Federal Building.

Ponca City   Bartlesville

Claremore •
Tulsa •   Tahlequah •

IT HAPPENED HERE:
On April 22, 1889, a shot rang out and settlers raced to stake a claim. By evening what is today called Oklahoma City had sprung up, its first twelve thousand inhabitants all living in tents.

OKLAHOMA CITY ★
Norman •
• Anadarko

Southern Plains Indian Museum, Anadarko

• Lawton

Duncan

Mickey Mantle, a powerful man at bat, grew up in Commerce.

Sixty-seven tribes are represented in Oklahoma. The Cherokees, Chickasaws, Choctaws, Creeks, and Seminoles, who resettled here from the east in the first half of the nineteenth century, compose more than half of the Native American population.

The Red Earth Festival, in Oklahoma City, celebrates Native American cultures.

Red River

7

Susanna Salter, of Argonia, became America's first woman mayor in 1887.

Turkey Red wheat, brought by Russian Mennonites in the 1870s, made Kansas the nation's leading producer of wheat.

Dwight Eisenhower, raised in Abilene, became the thirty-fourth president in 1953.

In The Wonderful Wizard of Oz, published by L. Frank Baum in 1900, a Kansas tornado sweeps Dorothy to the Land of Oz.

In 1950 poet Gwendolyn Brooks, born in Topeka, became the first African American to win the Pulitzer Prize.

Clyde Cessna, Walter Beech, and William Lear all launched pioneer aviation enterprises in Wichita.

★ KANSAS ★
STATEHOOD 1861

OZ Museum, Wamego

Buffalo Soldiers—African-American fighting men—are honored at Fort Leavenworth.

Nobel Prize winner Jack St. Clair Kilby, of Great Bend, invented the microchip in 1958.

Dear Grandpa, If you visit Dodge City's Front Street, you'll think you're in the Wild West days of Wyatt Earp. From, Ben

In 1932 Amelia Earhart, born in Atchison, was the first woman to fly solo across the Atlantic.

State bird: Western meadowlark

In the 1850s fighting over slavery led to the name Bleeding Kansas.

Atop the capitol dome is a statue of a Kansa Indian.

♪ "Oh, give me a home ♪♫♪ Where the buffalo roam..." ♪ —From the Kansas State song, "Home on the Range"

Kansas leads the nation in general aircraft production.

Called the "Father of Basketball Coaching," Forrest "Phog" Allen was coach at the University of Kansas for thirty-nine seasons.

World's largest ball of sisal twine, Cawker City

The geographic center of the forty-eight contiguous states is near Lebanon.

• Lebanon
• Cawker City
• Marysville
Atchison
Wamego• Leavenworth
Abilene •
TOPEKA ★ Kansas City
Emporia •
• Great Bend
Wichita •
Argonia •
Sedan • Independence

Castle Rock

Castle Rock, a limestone formation, was a landmark for pioneers headed west.

• Dodge City

World-renowned clown Emmett Kelly was born in Sedan in 1898.

Pony Express Home Station No. 1, in Marysville, was the first overnight stop on the Pony Express trail.

Botanica, a collection of gardens, is in Wichita, Kansas's largest city.

One of the windiest states, Kansas is in Tornado Alley, a swath of land that runs from Texas to Nebraska and has more tornadoes than any place else in the country.

IT HAPPENED HERE:
In Topeka in 1950 Oliver Brown decided his daughter Linda should not have to attend a segregated school. Four years later, in Brown v. Board of Education, the Supreme Court outlawed racial segregation in schools.

William Allen White, of Emporia, won a Pulitzer Prize for a 1922 editorial defending freedom of speech.

In 1929 Charles Curtis, of Topeka, became the first U.S. vice president of Native American descent.

State flower: Sunflower

Pulitzer Prize-winning playwright William Inge was born in Independence in 1913.

"Soddies"

Dear Grandpa,
Dad told us how pioneers heading west traveled the Platte River valley through Nebraska. When people came to stay, they built houses called soddies out of blocks of grassy earth. Sometimes bugs and snakes fell from the ceilings!
From, Ben

Scotts Bluff National Monument

To pioneers traveling across flat and treeless prairies, Courthouse and Jail Rocks, Chimney Rock, and Scotts Bluff were amazing sights. One traveler called Scotts Bluff "grand beyond description."

★ NEBRASKA ★
Chimney Rock
STATEHOOD 1867

State flower: Goldenrod

The proportion of land in Nebraska used to produce crops and livestock is greater than in any other state.

IT HAPPENED HERE:
In North Platte on July 4, 1882, Buffalo Bill Cody staged the Old Glory Blowout, a celebration so popular that it inspired him to create his famous Wild West show.

The Pawnees, the largest group of Indians living in this area when European explorers first arrived here, were among the Native Americans portrayed by artist George Catlin in 1832.

Dear Grandma,
You've got to try Nebraska steak and corn on the cob!
Love, Annie

Scotts Bluff National Monument
Chimney Rock National Historic Site
State bird: Western meadowlark

North Platte · Norfolk
Platte River · Grand Island · LINCOLN · Omaha · Bellevue
Red Cloud · Wilbur · Nebraska City · Beatrice
Missouri River

One of America's great novelists, Willa Cather, of Red Cloud, wrote about the hopes and hardships of pioneer life.

In 1945, after Nebraska's football team was dubbed the Cornhuskers, the legislature voted to call Nebraska the Cornhusker State.

Willa Cather on a railroad handcar.

Gardens and a conservation center honor the Omaha birth site of thirty-eighth president Gerald Ford.

Dancer Fred Astaire and activist Malcolm X were born in Omaha. Entertainer Johnny Carson grew up in Norfolk.

Susan La Flesche Picotte, of the Omaha Nation, was the first Native American woman to earn a medical degree.

Mammoth fossils have been discovered in most Nebraska counties.

Boys Town, established by Father Edward Flanagan in Omaha in 1917 to help neglected boys, is today called Girls and Boys Town.

Fairview, home of congressman, secretary of state, and famed orator William Jennings Bryan, is in Lincoln.

Celebrating Arbor Day

Early settlers in Nebraska planted millions of trees. In 1872 J. Sterling Morton, of Nebraska City, proposed a holiday called Arbor Day to celebrate tree planting.

The National Museum of Roller Skating, in Lincoln, honors skaters like Jesse Darling, famous in the early twentieth century, and her skating partner, Henry Simmons.

"I realized that all the really good ideas I'd ever had came to me while I was milking a cow. So I went back to Iowa." – Painter Grant Wood

Iowa leads the nation in corn production. More than a food, corn is used to make everything from crayons to firecrackers to fuel.

State bird: Eastern goldfinch

IOWA
STATEHOOD 1846

State flower: Wild rose

Amelia Bloomer promoted pants for women, which came to be known as bloomers. She was also head of the Iowa Woman Suffrage Association.

The town of Pella, settled by the Dutch, celebrates the Tulip Time festival in May.

In 1788 French Canadian Julien Dubuque became the first white settler in Iowa.

Fort Des Moines was the site of the army's first training program for African-American officers during World War I and for the first women officers during World War II.

Iowa's state capitol building has one gold and four copper domes.

alex. there are about five hogs for every person in iowa. that's a lotta pork! ben

The Roseman Covered Bridge, near Winterset, was featured in the novel and movie The Bridges of Madison County and is one of five covered bridges in the county.

Big-band leader Glenn Miller was born in Clarinda.

Born in Mason City, Meredith Willson modeled River City, the town in his musical The Music Man, after his hometown.

Prehistoric people began building the mounds in Effigy Mounds National Monument more than 1,400 years ago. Of the 195 mounds 31 are in the shapes of animals.

American Gothic house, Eldon, site of Grant Wood's famous painting

Born in Waterloo, First Lady Lou Hoover loved to hike and camp. Through decades-long work with the Girl Scouts, she helped others to know the joys of outdoor life.

Dear Grandma,
At the Chocolate Haus, in the Amana Colonies (which were settled by German immigrants), we had fudge and chocolate truffles, made same as in the olden days. Liebe (that's "love" in German), Annie

Actor John Wayne was born in a four-room house in Winterset.

A plant in Cedar Rapids manufactures Quaker Oats.

Thirty-first president Herbert Hoover was born in this West Branch home in 1874.

Black Hawk, a Sauk warrior, resisted U.S. government efforts to drive the Sauk and Mesquakie Indians from their lands. Many people believe that the state's nickname, the Hawkeye State, was devised as a tribute to him.

Map labels: Mason City, Sioux City, Missouri River, Effigy Mounds National Monument, Dubuque, Waterloo, Cedar Rapids, West Branch, Davenport, DES MOINES, Amana Colonies, Council Bluffs, Winterset, Pella, Clarinda, Eldon, Mississippi River

QUAKER OATS

Artichoke Lake · Pickle Lake · Bear Head Lake · Pug Hole Lake · Bladder Lake · Pigs Eye Lake · Dirty Nose Lake · Leech Lake · Lake Full of Fish · Big Ole Lake

Devil Track Lake · Mille Lacs Lake · Otter Tail Lake · Potato Lake · Stump Lake · Big Bishke Muncie Lake · Spunk Lake · Foot Lake · Grave Lake · Coffin Lake · O'Leary Lake

Mud Lake · Upper Red Lake · Heikkila Lake · Moses Lake · Lake Winnibigoshish · Spoon Lake · Lake One · Lake Two · Knaus Lake · Fire Lake · Little Dead Horse Lake

Egg Lake · Mantrap Lake · Wagner Lake · Sock Lake · Swede Lake · Hand Lake · Split Lake · Kolstad Lake · Skunk Lake · Ball Club Lake · Big Bird Lake · Kabetogama Lake · Minnow Lake

In the eighteenth century French-Canadian fur traders, called voyageurs, traveled Minnesota waters and traded with the Ojibwa and Dakota Indians.

Minnesota, nicknamed Land of 10,000 Lakes, actually has nearly 12,000 of them, and most have names.

Dear Grandma,
At Lake Itasca, the headwaters of the Mississippi, the river starts out as a shallow stream. It's good luck to cross it, and I did!
Love, Annie

State flower: Showy lady's slipper

State bird: Common loon

MINNESOTA · STATEHOOD 1858
Split Rock Lighthouse, Two Harbors

The Mayo Clinic, which draws patients from around the world, grew out of the Rochester medical practice started by frontier doctor William Mayo and his two sons.

alex. annie got her head examined with one of the quack medical devices in the science museum. they didn't find anything. (kidding!) ben

Minnesotan Charles Schulz created the Peanuts comic strip.

The Judy Garland Museum is in the house in Grand Rapids where she first lived.

Psycograph, Science Museum of Minnesota, St. Paul

Minnehaha Falls, located in a park in Minneapolis, was made famous by Henry Wadsworth Longfellow's 1855 poem, The Song of Hiawatha.

Guthrie Theater

Minneapolis is known for its theaters and theater companies.

The Bakken, a museum in Minneapolis, chronicles the history of electricity.

The Bakken

Most of the nation's iron ore, which is used to make steel, comes from the Mesabi Iron Range.

State fish: Walleye

The nation's largest mall, the Mall of America, in Bloomington, houses an indoor amusement park.

Minnesota is the top turkey-producing state.

Paul Bunyan and Babe the blue ox, Bemidji

St. Paul was originally called Pig's Eye Landing.

Fort Snelling, restored today as a historic landmark in St. Paul, was a U.S. Army outpost in the nineteenth century and a gathering spot for Native Americans and traders.

When Sinclair Lewis, who grew up in Sauk Centre, won the Nobel Prize in Literature in 1930, he became the first American to do so.

Spoonbridge and Cherry, by Claes Oldenburg and Coosje van Bruggen, is in the Minneapolis Sculpture Garden.

Jolly Green Giant statue, in Blue Earth

Minneapolis, the largest city, and St. Paul, the capital, are called the Twin Cities.

Minneapolis · Stone Arch Bridge

Author of the classic novel The Great Gatsby, F. Scott Fitzgerald was born in St. Paul.

Voyageurs National Park · Bemidji · Lake Itasca · Mesabi Iron Range · Boundary Waters Canoe Area Wilderness · Eagle Mountain · Grand Rapids · Two Harbors · Lake Superior · Duluth · Mississippi River · St. Paul · Sauk Centre · Minneapolis · Bloomington · Blue Earth · Rochester

State bird:
Western meadowlark

Walleye

Dakota Skipper

Northern Pike

Ring-necked pheasant

"As the sun angled, the buttes and coulees, the cliffs and sculptured hills and ravines...glowed with...a hundred variations of red and silver gray....I can easily see how people are driven back to the Bad Lands." —John Steinbeck

State flower: Wild prairie rose

NORTH DAKOTA

The Badlands

STATEHOOD 1889

Bison

Annie spots a flickertail squirrel.

Jamestown is the birthplace of singer-songwriter Peggy Lee and American West author Louis L'Amour.

Mule deer

North Dakota has sixty-two wildlife refuges, more than any other state.

The Red River of the North flows north, setting it apart from most large U.S. rivers.

Hereford cow

Moose

Nearly a third of North Dakotans are of Norwegian descent. Norsk Høstfest, a yearly festival in Minot, celebrates Scandinavian heritage.

International Peace Garden

Minot

Lake Sakakawea

Warsaw

Red River of the North

Saint Joseph's Chapel, near Warsaw, is one of the smallest in America.

White-tailed jackrabbit

Grand Forks

Elk

IT HAPPENED HERE:
In 1804, while Meriwether Lewis and William Clark were at Fort Mandan, Sakakawea joined their expedition to the Pacific.

U.S. Hockey Hall of Famer Cliff "Fido" Purpur, of Grand Forks

Theodore Roosevelt National Park

Badlands

Missouri River

Fort Mandan

Fargo

Red fox

Dear Grandpa,
The International Peace Garden is partly in Canada and partly in the U.S., so I stood with a foot in each country!
From, Ben

Regent

BISMARCK

Jamestown

The Fargo Theatre, once a vaudeville playhouse, is a movie palace today.

FARGO

Bighorn sheep

Pronghorn antelope

alex. along the enchanted highway an artisan from regent has built giant metal sculptures. ben

Coyote

Nokota horse

Northern leopard frog

Prairie dogs

Long-tailed weasel

Raccoon

Pelican

Dorset lamb

"We have come here to dedicate a cornerstone that was laid by the hand of the Almighty."—President Coolidge, 1927, Mount Rushmore dedication

Avenue of Flags, Mount Rushmore

Standing Rock Reservation

A monument marks the grave of Sitting Bull, a spiritual leader of the Sioux, in the Standing Rock Reservation.

Deadwood, a legendary gambling town during early gold rush days, is where Wild Bill Hickok met his end. He was shot while playing poker.

Aberdeen

The exterior walls of the Corn Palace, in Mitchell, are decorated each year with corn, grain, grasses, and wild oats, following a custom started by early settlers, who wanted to show the abundance of their harvest.

In 1964 Billy Mills, who grew up on the Pine Ridge Reservation, won Olympic gold in the 10,000-meter run.

Deadwood
Black Hills National Forest
Rapid City
Crazy Horse Memorial
Mount Rushmore National Monument
Pine Ridge Reservation
Badlands National Park
Wounded Knee Battlefield
Pierre
Missouri River
Mitchell
Sioux Falls
State flower: Pasque flower
Vermillion

South Dakota is a leading gold producer.

IT HAPPENED HERE:
In December 1890, U.S. cavalrymen surrounded fleeing Sioux at Wounded Knee Creek and tried to disarm them. A gun went off, and the soldiers started firing, killing at least 150 Sioux.

alex. the butterflies are so friendly at the sertoma butterfly house in sioux falls. ben

Crazy Horse fiercely resisted efforts to move the Lakotas onto reservations. Sculptor Korczak Ziolkowski began this memorial to him in 1948.

SOUTH DAKOTA
Crazy Horse Memorial
★ STATEHOOD 1889 ★

Reptile Gardens, south of Rapid City

In 1935, outside Rapid City, a manned balloon, the Explorer II, ascended to 72,395 feet, high enough to see the curvature of the earth.

State bird: Ring-necked pheasant

As many as sixty million buffalo once roamed North America's grasslands, but by 1900 only about a thousand survived. Ranchers like South Dakotan Scotty Philip began raising them, and slowly their numbers increased. There are some eight thousand buffalo in South Dakota today.

Dear Grandma,
At the National Music Museum, in Vermillion, we saw rare and unusual instruments, like the "trumpet organ." Love, Annie

Chief Plenty Coups, a brave warrior of the Crow Nation, urged cooperation with white settlers.

State flower: Bitterroot

Janine Pease, the first woman of Crow ancestry to earn a PhD, has worked to bring educational opportunities to Native Americans.

On the ceiling of the capitol rotunda, in Helena, paintings of four figures represent Montana's history: a Native American, an explorer/trapper, a prospector, and a cowboy.

Jeannette Rankin, born near Missoula, was the first woman member of the U.S. House of Representatives. She represented Montana from 1917 to 1919 and from 1941 to 1943.

State bird: Western meadowlark

Fort Benton, known as the birthplace of Montana, was established as a fur trading post in 1846. o Fort Benton

"Overhead there was more sky than a man could think, curving deep and far and empty, except maybe for a hawk or an eagle sailing." —A.B. Guthrie Jr.

"The Bob"

A dinosaur dig near Egg Mountain, where nests of dinosaur eggs have been found

alex. there are grizzly bears bigger than dad in the bob (which is what the locals call the bob marshall wilderness). the ben

Wm Clark July 25 1806

The Continental Divide is formed by the crest of the Rocky Mountains. Waters on one side flow east; on the other, west.

Glacier National Park
Rocky Mountains
Continental Divide
Egg Mountain
Choteau
Bob Marshall Wilderness
Fort Benton
Great Falls
Missoula
HELENA
Grant-Kohrs Ranch NHS
Butte
Bannack
Jefferson
Madison
Gallatin
Pompeys Pillar National Monument
Billings
Seventh Cavalry Monument
Little Bighorn Battlefield
Missouri River

The art of Montanan Charles M. Russell captures the spirit of the Old West.

IT HAPPENED HERE: In 1876 at a battle near the Little Bighorn River, Cheyenne and Sioux warriors overwhelmed and killed Lt. Col. George Armstrong Custer and more than two hundred soldiers of the Seventh Cavalry.

A. B. Guthrie Jr., who grew up in Choteau, wrote a 1947 novel, The Big Sky, which gave Montana its nickname: Big Sky Country.

The Big Sky
The Way West

Movie stars Myrna Loy and Gary Cooper were from Montana.

William Clark's inscription on Pompeys Pillar is the only remaining physical evidence of the Lewis and Clark expedition along the route. Clark named the sandstone butte Pompeys Tower after Sakakawea's child, whom he called Pomp.

Dear Grandma,
In Fort Benton we saw the statue of Shep, a dog whose master died and was sent back east for burial. The faithful dog greeted every train for five years, expecting his master's return.
Love, Annie

Grant-Kohrs Ranch National Historic Site shows how cowboys lived.

In 1932 the spectacular Going-to-the-Sun Road was completed. It goes through Glacier National Park.

MONTANA
Going-to-the-Sun Road
STATEHOOD 1889

After the discovery of both silver and copper there, Butte Hill became known as the "richest hill on earth."

Bannack was Montana's first town, built during the gold rush. o Now a ghost town.

Explorer and trapper John Colter left the Lewis and Clark expedition as it was on its homeward journey, and in 1807-8 explored what is now Yellowstone National Park. Other fur trappers who followed described an amazing place of geysers and boiling pools, but their accounts were dismissed as tall tales. In 1871 Thomas Moran and William Jackson, members of an expedition led by geologist Ferdinand Hayden, painted and photographed the region's wonders, and in 1872 Yellowstone became the first national park.

alex. i finished the requirements for becoming a yellowstone junior ranger by hiking mystic falls trail. that's six patches i've earned. ben

Dear Grandma,
Josh said "Awesome!" when we first saw the Morning Glory Pool at Yellowstone National Park. I got a set of National Parks postcards, which I'll write to you so that you can see awesome sights too.
Love, Annie

DENALI National Park and Preserve

GRAND CANYON National Park

ZION NATIONAL PARK

GLACIER NATIONAL PARK

CRATER LAKE National Park

National Park

WIZARD ISLAND

VOLCANOES NATIONAL PARK

HALEAKALA

EVERGLADES National Park

MOUNT RAINIER National

JUNIOR RANGER YELLOWSTONE

ACADIA NATIONAL PARK

GETTYSBURG NATIONAL MILITARY PARK

MAMMOTH CAVE

SEQUOIA NATIONAL PARK

GREAT SMOKY MOUNTAINS National Park

ARCHES National Park

YOSEMITE EL CAPITAN

Elk antler arch, Jackson

BUFFALO BILL'S WILD WEST

The Buffalo Bill Historical Center, in Cody, is five museums, including one about Plains Indians and another of Western art.

Chief Washakie, leader of the Shoshone people by 1850, remained chief until his death in 1900.

WYOMING
The Tetons
★ STATEHOOD 1890 ★

An outdoorsman and the husband of the author of this book, Vice President Dick Cheney grew up in Casper.

alex, dude—the eatons started the first dude ranch near sheridan. tourists have been coming to this ranch since 1904. ben

In 1906 Devils Tower, more than a thousand feet tall, became the country's first national monument. President Theodore Roosevelt signed the proclamation.

Jackson Pollock, born in Cody, revolutionized American painting in the 1940s and '50s.

The National Historic Trails Interpretive Center, in Casper, has exhibits that show how the pioneers traveled and how the trails they followed—the Oregon, California, and Mormon Trails—all crossed the Rocky Mountains at South Pass.

Pioneer woman driving a grain binder

In Letters of a Woman Homesteader, Elinore Pruitt Stewart describes what life was like for early twentieth-century pioneers.

Map labels:
Yellowstone National Park
Cody
Sheridan
Devils Tower National Monument
The Grand Teton
Snake River
Jackson
Thermopolis
Gillette
Continental Divide
Riverton
Lander
Casper
Pinedale
South Pass
Independence Rock
Great Divide Basin
Rock Springs
North Platte River
Laramie
CHEYENNE

There are more than 280 prehistoric drawings preserved at the Legend Rock Petroglyph Site, near Thermopolis.

Wyoming is the nation's number one coal producer.

IT HAPPENED HERE:
In 1869 in Cheyenne the territorial legislature passed a law making Wyoming the first in the nation to recognize full voting rights for women.

Jade, the state gemstone, is mined near Lander.

Thousands of pioneers bound for California, Utah, and Oregon left signatures on Independence Rock.

State bird: Meadowlark

State flower: Indian paintbrush

WELCOME TO INDEPENDENCE ROCK
WYOMING STATE PARKS AND HISTORIC SITES

The Museum of the Mountain Man, in Pinedale, explains the early Rocky Mountain fur trade and the lives of men like trapper and scout Jim Bridger.

Louisa Swain — 1870: 1st woman to vote in Wyoming

Esther Hobart Morris — 1870: 1st woman judicial officer

Nellie Tayloe Ross — 1925: 1st woman governor

Dear Grandma,
Do you know what's called the Daddy of 'em All? The Frontier Days rodeo, in Cheyenne. And guess what's cool even though it's really warm: my mountain man hat.
Love, Annie

The Black American West Museum and Heritage Center, in Denver, portrays the contributions of African-American pioneers, like mountain man Jim Beckwourth.

Colorado has more than two dozen ski resorts.

Born in 1871 in a Colorado mining town, Dr. Florence Sabin was a noted medical researcher and a pioneer in public health reform.

Colorado is the highest state, with more than a thousand Rocky Mountain peaks over ten thousand feet high; fifty-four are "fourteeners," or over fourteen thousand feet high.

Colorado is the fittest state, according to one survey. Its residents have three hundred days of sunshine to exercise outdoors.

Chief Ouray sought land and peace for the Ute people when gold prospectors came onto their land.

The more than six billion coins made at the U.S. Mint in Denver each year are marked with a D.

When prospectors began rushing to Colorado for gold in 1858, they kept an eye out for Pikes Peak, the easternmost of the big Rocky Mountain peaks. "Pikes Peak or Bust" became their slogan.

Dear Grandma,
Denver is a mile high, and so water boils at a lower temperature here, which means you have to cook a boiled egg longer. I decided to have a Denver omelet instead.
Love,
Annie

Dinosaur National Monument

State flower: White and lavender columbine

"For purple mountain majesties above the fruited plain!"

Boulder
DENVER
Aurora
Vail
Leadville
Aspen
Colorado River
Grand Junction
Rocky Mountains
Pikes Peak
Garden of the Gods
Cheyenne Mountain
Colorado Springs
Royal Gorge Bridge
Continental Divide
Telluride
Mesa Verde National Park
Four Corners Monument
Manassa

IT HAPPENED HERE:
In 1893 Katharine Lee Bates traveled to Colorado. The view from the top of Pikes Peak inspired her to write a poem she entitled "America the Beautiful."

The Colorado Ski Museum, in Vail, tells how veterans of the Tenth Mountain Division helped make skiing a popular sport.

The Tony Awards are named after Antoinette Perry, born in Denver, who was an avid supporter of the theater.

After Coloradan Margaret Brown survived the sinking of the Titanic, she became known as "the Unsinkable Molly Brown."

One of forty-four chiefs of the Northern Cheyenne Tribe, Ben Nighthorse Campbell represented Colorado in the U.S. Senate from 1993 to 2005.

alex. we're at four corners monument—the only spot in the u.s. where four states meet: colorado, new mexico, arizona, and utah. ben

State bird: Lark bunting

Four Corners Monument

Colorado is called the Centennial State because it became the thirty-eighth state the year of America's one hundredth birthday.

COLORADO
STATEHOOD 1876
Balanced Rock
Garden of the Gods

In 1881 Helen Hunt Jackson, who lived in Colorado Springs, published A Century of Dishonor. It documents poor treatment of Native Americans.

In the 1880s Leadville's silver mines created overnight millionaires.

From Manassa, Jack Dempsey was heavyweight boxing champion of the world from 1919 to 1926.

Constructed on giant springs within Cheyenne Mountain, the operations center of the North American Aerospace Defense Command (NORAD) was built to withstand nuclear attack.

The Anasazi, a Puebloan people, built the cliff dwellings at Mesa Verde National Park more than seven hundred years ago.

Honoring his adopted state, singer-songwriter John Denver changed his last name from Deutschendorf and wrote the song "Rocky Mountain High."

The Cadet Chapel

The state capitol has a dome leafed with gold and an interior built with Colorado rose onyx.

The Royal Gorge Bridge is the highest suspension bridge in the world, at 1,053 feet above the Arkansas River.

The U.S. Air Force Academy, established in 1954, moved to its Colorado Springs location in 1958.

In 1908 George McJunkin, an African-American cowboy, discovered a bone pit near Folsom that would revolutionize the scientific thinking of the time by proving that humans had been in North America at least ten thousand years.

The Albuquerque International Balloon Fiesta, held each fall, is the largest balloon event in the world.

The high mountains and desert around Santa Fe, Abiquiu, and Taos inspired artist Georgia O'Keeffe.

NEW MEXICO
STATEHOOD 1912

Santa Fe, which became the capital of the Spanish province of New Mexico in 1610, is the oldest of our nation's state capitals.

San Miguel Mission, Santa Fe

San Miguel Mission is the oldest church in U.S. still in use.

Visiting an Anasazi dwelling, Bandelier National Monument

State bird: Roadrunner

State flower: Yucca

Zuni Pueblo, the largest of New Mexico's pueblos, is home to more than six thousand.

Four Corners Monument

The National Atomic Museum, in Albuquerque, presents the history of the atomic age, including the development of the first two nuclear weapons, which were built in Los Alamos and used to end World War II in 1945.

Ship Rock

Chaco Culture National Historical Park

Abiquiu
Taos
Los Alamos
San Ildefonso Pueblo
Bandelier National Monument
SANTA FE

Gallup
Zuni

Folsom

Remember—Only you can PREVENT FOREST FIRES!

Maria Martinez, of San Ildefonso Pueblo, worked with her husband, Julian, to create pottery that is much prized today.

Trinity Site marks the place where an atomic bomb was first tested and the nuclear age began.

Albuquerque

Continental Divide

IT HAPPENED HERE: In 1950 soldiers saved a bear cub after a fire in the Lincoln National Forest. The cub, later called Smokey Bear, became the symbol of preventing forest fires.

Dear Grandma,
In New Mexico they have a state cookie, the bizcochito. It's yummy and crunchy and tastes like licorice.
Love, Annie

Dear Grandpa,
We learned the amazing story of the Navajo "code talkers," who served as U.S. Marine communicators during World War II. By using their language, they were able to send messages that Japanese code breakers couldn't break!
From, Ben

Rio Grande

Trinity Site

Lincoln National Forest
Roswell
UFO Museum, Roswell

Alamogordo

New Mexico is the number one U.S. producer of chiles.

White Sands National Monument

Las Cruces

Carlsbad Caverns

In 1935 Dennis Chávez became the first American-born Hispanic U.S. senator.

HAM the astrochimp helped pave the way for astronauts when he traveled into space in 1961. He is buried at the New Mexico Museum of Space History, in Alamogordo.

On the floor of the capitol building is an image that combines the sun symbol of Zia Pueblo with the state seal of New Mexico, which shows a large eagle shielding a smaller one.

"The glories and the beauties of form, color, and sound unite in the Grand Canyon." ~John Wesley Powell

Named after a bird that rises from its ashes, the city of Phoenix arose when settlers extended a system of canals laid out by the ancient Hohokam people. Today Phoenix is the nation's sixth largest city.

Dear Grandma,
Arizona is the only state with official state neckwear: the bola tie. Don't tell Grandpa, but we bought him one.
Love, Annie

alex. after 131 years of spanning the thames river, london bridge was taken apart and rebuilt at lake havasu. ben

Lettuce, cotton, and cantaloupe are top crops in Arizona.

Grand Canyon National Park

Hoover Dam

Colorado River

Lake Havasu City

London Bridge

Prescott

Monument Valley

Four Corners Monument

Navajo Reservation

Hopi Reservation

Flagstaff

Canyon de Chelly National Monument

IT HAPPENED HERE:
In 1930 Clyde Tombaugh discovered the planet Pluto at Lowell Observatory, in Flagstaff.

Arizonan Sandra Day O'Connor became the first woman justice of the U.S. Supreme Court in 1981.

Scottsdale
Mesa
PHOENIX

Tucson

Chiricahua National Monument

Kitt Peak National Observatory

Tombstone

In 1869 John Wesley Powell led the first expedition to travel the uncharted canyons of the Colorado River.

Canyon de Chelly, where Anasazi once built cliff dwellings, is home to Navajos today.

In the 1930s Frank Lloyd Wright established Taliesin West, in Scottsdale, as his winter home, studio, and architectural school.

ARIZONA
Phoenix
STATEHOOD 1912

With telescopes on nearby Kitt Peak, Mount Hopkins, and Mount Graham, Tucson is sometimes called the Astronomy Capital of the World.

State bird: Cactus wren
State flower: Saguaro cactus blossom

The Gila monster, a large venomous lizard, lives in the Arizona desert.

The Heard Museum, in Phoenix, displays Native American art, including Hopi katsina dolls.

Arizona leads the nation in copper production.

Apache leader Geronimo fought fiercely for his people before surrendering to the U.S. Army in 1886.

Prescott Frontier Days

State insect: Honeybee

★ UTAH ★

Rainbow Bridge

STATEHOOD 1896

In 1848 swarms of crickets were destroying crops, until seagulls arrived and ate them, thus saving pioneers from starving during their first year in Utah.

State bird: Seagull

State flower: Sego lily

Floating in the Great Salt Lake

Rainbow Bridge, by Lake Powell, is the world's largest natural bridge.

IT HAPPENED HERE: On May 10, 1869, the Union Pacific railway met the Central Pacific railway at Promontory Summit, creating the first transcontinental railroad.

Pioneer Day, July 24, commemorates the arrival of the Mormons in the Salt Lake Valley.

The Salt Lake Temple of the LDS Church, finished in 1893, is in Temple Square.

Park City hosts the Sundance Film Festival each January.

Promontory

Great Salt Lake

Bonneville Salt Flats

THE BLUE FLAME

SALT LAKE CITY

Park City
West Valley City
Provo

Dinosaur National Monument

alex. in 1970 gary gabelich drove a rocket-powered car, the "blue flame," 622.4 mph on the bonneville salt flats. ben

In 1896 Martha Hughes Cannon, a doctor, was elected the first woman state senator. One of her opponents in the election was her husband.

The Dinosaur Quarry Visitor Center encloses some fifteen hundred dinosaur bones.

Uinta Mountains

Born in Beaver County, Philo Farnsworth invented basic components of electronic television.

At Arches National Park thousands of arches and spires rise out of the desert.

Bryce Canyon, a maze of rock formations, was named after pioneer Ebenezer Bryce. He observed it was not a place you would want to lose a cow.

Moab

Canyonlands National Park

Colorado River

Utah's natural resources include petroleum, coal, and copper.

Bryce Canyon National Park

Grand Staircase-Escalante National Monument

Lake Powell

Rainbow Bridge National Monument

Four Corners Monument

Dear Grandma,
The pipe organ that accompanies the world-famous Mormon Tabernacle Choir has 11,623 pipes!
Love, Annie

Built by members of the Coeur d'Alene tribe and Catholic missionaries between 1848 and 1853, the Cataldo Mission is the oldest standing building in Idaho.

Visitors can dig and pan for star garnets—the state's official gem—at the Emerald Creek Garnet Area.

IDAHO
Sawtooth Mountains
STATEHOOD 1890

World Center for Birds of Prey, Boise

More than one billion ounces of silver have been produced in northern Idaho's Silver Valley.

Coeur d'Alene

Emerald Creek Garnet Area

Moscow

At its deepest point Hells Canyon is deeper than the Grand Canyon.

Hells Canyon

State flower: Syringa

alex. golden eagles can go 200 mph when diving after prey. ben

Dear Grandma,
I caught a giant cutthroat trout at Henrys Fork of the Snake River. (Well, Dad helped a little.) Then we carefully put it back.
Love, Annie

The first chairlift, based on technology used to hoist bananas onto ships, was built at the Sun Valley ski resort in 1936.

Sawtooth Range

Sun Valley ski resort

Rexburg

Henrys Fork

Carol Ryrie Brink, born in Moscow, Idaho, wrote the 1936 Newbery Medal–winning children's book, Caddie Woodlawn.

Nampa

★ BOISE

Ketchum

Idaho Falls

Blackfoot

Pocatello

Snake River

Craters of the Moon National Monument and Preserve

Balanced Rock

Helped by the Shoshones, Meriwether Lewis and William Clark explored this region in 1805. Canadian fur traders followed and set up trading posts. In 1860, the year that Mormons established the first permanent settlement, gold was discovered, bringing thousands of miners into the region.

Powering instruments on the ten-year space mission to Pluto, launched in 2006, is a plutonium battery produced at the Idaho National Laboratory.

Idaho ranks first in potato production, growing almost a third of the nation's crop.

Balanced Rock

More than forty-eight feet tall, Balanced Rock stands on a base that is three feet by seventeen inches.

Craters of the Moon

The lava-covered landscape of Craters of the Moon National Monument and Preserve resembles the surface of the moon.

Appaloosa horses, long bred by the Nez Percés, were admired by Lewis and Clark.

State bird: Mountain bluebird

J. R. Simplot's company developed frozen french fries and instant mashed potatoes. He also helped start Micron Technology, based in Boise, which makes computer chips.

IDAHO Potatoes U.S. #1

In 1859 the richest deposit of silver ore in U.S. history was found east of the Sierra Nevada. The Comstock Lode, named after a miner who claimed the land was his, caused a rush to Virginia City and yielded almost $400 million in silver and gold before the lode was depleted. New discoveries of silver and gold brought a second, short-lived boom in the early twentieth century. Mining activity that began in the 1980s has led to Nevada's being the nation's leading producer of gold and silver today.

Dear Grandpa,
The famous writer Mark Twain was a Virginia City reporter in the boomtown days of the 1860s. There's a lifelike statue of him in a Virginia City bookstore.
From, Ben

Black Rock Desert

In the Black Rock Desert hot water erupts from geysers.

State flower: sagebrush

Joshua trees

Lake Tahoe, with shorelines in both Nevada and California, is one of the world's deepest lakes.

Lake Tahoe

Black Rock Desert

Winnemucca

State bird: Mountain bluebird

The daughter of a chief, Sarah Winnemucca sought to right the wrongs her people had suffered, most notably with her 1883 book, Life Among the Piutes.

alex. the nevada desert has interesting plants: sagebrush, joshua trees, and bristlecones, which are the oldest living trees on the planet. ben

Ancient bristlecone pines

Reno
Virginia City
★ CARSON CITY

Lake Tahoe

Great Basin National Park

Hoover Dam

RENO
THE BIGGEST LITTLE CITY IN THE WORLD

Bottle House

Sierra Nevada

Rhyolite

Rhyolite, a ghost town today, was a gold rush boomtown in 1906, when miner Tom Kelly built a house there of fifty thousand bottles.

Hot August Nights, in Reno, is a celebration of classic cars.

Coins from the Carson City mint, closed in 1893, are marked CC. Today the mint building houses the Nevada State Museum.

Nevada's crops include garlic, alfalfa seed, and mint.

Hoover Dam, on the border of Nevada and Arizona, is one of the world's great engineering marvels.

Valley of Fire State Park
Lake Mead
Las Vegas
Henderson
Hoover Dam
Laughlin

Before she died in 1925, a Washoe woman named Dat-So-La-Lee became one of the most famous basket weavers in the world.

VIVA! Las Vegas
ALAD

Las Vegas

A small railroad town at the beginning of the twentieth century, Las Vegas today draws tourists from around the world.

Dear Grandma,
In Vegas we went to the Liberace Museum and saw his famous rhinestone-covered piano, costumes, and car. Dazzling!
Love, Annie

NEVADA
★ ★
STATEHOOD 1864
Elephant Rock

In Valley of Fire State Park, where Elephant Rock is located, the sandstone glows a fiery red at certain times of day.

Before 1542: About one hundred Native American tribes inhabit the region.

Paiutes

1542: Juan Rodríguez Cabrillo leads the first European expedition to California.

1769: Missionary Junípero Serra founds the first of twenty-one missions: Mission San Diego de Alcalá.

1776: Mission San Francisco de Asís is founded; it's the oldest structure in San Francisco today.

In California, home to many ethnic groups—including non-Hispanic whites, Hispanics, Asians, Pacific Islanders, African Americans, and Native Americans—no single group constitutes a majority.

★ CALIFORNIA ★
San Francisco
STATEHOOD 1850

California is the nation's leading agricultural state.

Ninety percent of U.S. wine is produced in California.

The Asian Art Museum of San Francisco encourages appreciation of the art and culture of Asia.

1976: Steven Jobs and Stephen Wozniak start Apple Computer in a garage in Los Altos, near Palo Alto.

In the 1960s the Beach Boys captured the California feeling with hits like "California Girls."

State bird: California valley quail

GRACE KELLY
Hollywood Walk of Fame

Movie star Mary Pickford, who won an Academy Award in 1929, was a founder of United Artists film studio.

1962: César Chávez begins organizing farmworkers to seek better pay and working conditions.

Isadora Duncan, born in San Francisco in 1878, was a modern-dance innovator.

In the La Brea Tar Pits, in downtown Los Angeles, paleontologists are still finding fossils of animals that lived in California many thousands of years ago.

State flower: California poppy

SHRINE DRIVE-THRU TREE
AGE 5000 HEIGHT 275 FT.
DIA. 21 FT. CIR. 64 FT.
MYERS FLAT, CALIFORNIA

Shrine Drive-Thru Tree, Myers Flat

1955: Walt Disney opens Disneyland in a 160-acre orange grove in Anaheim.

Dear Grandma,
On Olvera Street in Los Angeles, I got you a Mexican painted angel. Josh had real Mexican food for the first time, and now he wants it for every meal!
Adios, Annie

In 1862 B'nai B'rith was the first Jewish congregation in Los Angeles. This Wilshire Boulevard synogogue has been the congregation's home since 1929.

1941–45: A factory in Long Beach builds planes, many by women, to support World War II.

1937: The Golden Gate Bridge, spanning the Golden Gate—the entrance to San Francisco Bay—is completed.

WINGS
CLARA BOW

1929: The silent movie Wings wins the first best picture Academy Award. The ceremony is held at the Hollywood Roosevelt Hotel.

HOLLYWOODLAND

1923: The Hollywoodland sign is erected in Hollywood Hills by a real estate developer. The sign will eventually be shortened to HOLLYWOOD.

1781: Governor Felipe de Neve brings forty-four settlers from Mexico to establish the pueblo that will become Los Angeles.

1834: Mexico distributes mission lands to Californios, Spanish-Mexican colonists.

1846: Declaring California independent of Mexico, about thirty Americans raise a flag with a bear on it.

1848: James Marshall discovers gold at Sutter's Mill, sparking the California gold rush of 1849.

1848: The Treaty of Guadalupe Hidalgo cedes California to the United States.

John Steinbeck, born in Salinas, won the Pulitzer Prize for his 1939 novel, The Grapes of Wrath.

Redwood National Park

Trees hundreds of feet tall live in Redwood National Park.

Eureka

Myers Flat

Yosemite Falls, the highest in the continent, has three drops, which fall a total of 2,425 feet.

The black-and-white photographs of Ansel Adams, born in San Francisco in 1902, capture the natural beauty of the American West.

1850s: Thousands of Chinese immigrants become part of the gold rush.

Among California's renowned universities are Stanford, the California Institute of Technology, and the University of California at Berkeley.

alex. at alcatraz we saw the cell block where infamous gangsters, like al capone, were held. spooky! ben

Chico

Yuba City

Lake Tahoe

Sutter's Mill

Stanford Union, Palo Alto

SACRAMENTO

Golden Gate Bridge

Berkeley

Alcatraz

San Francisco

Palo Alto

San Jose

Sierra Nevada

Yosemite National Park

The Ronald Reagan Presidential Library and Museum is in Simi Valley.

The library and museum of thirty-seventh president Richard Nixon is in Yorba Linda.

Circa 1873: The U.S. Department of Agriculture sends three small orange trees to Eliza Tibbets to plant in California soil.

Built by newspaper mogul William Randolph Hearst, Hearst Castle, in San Simeon, was designed by Californian Julia Morgan, a pioneer for women in architecture. She began work on the project in 1919.

Salinas

Monterey

Big Sur

San Simeon

Manzanar National Historic Site preserves the first permanent World War II internment camp for Japanese Americans.

Manzanar National Historic Site

Mount Whitney

Death Valley National Park

Mount Whitney is the tallest mountain in the forty-eight contiguous states. And at 282 feet below sea level, nearby Badwater Basin, in Death Valley, is the lowest point in the Western Hemisphere.

IT HAPPENED HERE:
In 1902 in Los Angeles, Thomas Tally opened his Electric Theatre, the first theater specifically for movies.

Santa Monica Pier, oldest pleasure pier on the West Coast

HISTORIC CALIFORNIA US 66 ROUTE

Needles

Santa Barbara

Santa Monica

Long Beach

Pacific Ocean

Simi Valley

Pasadena

Los Angeles

Yorba Linda

Anaheim

Palm Springs

San Juan Capistrano

Santa Catalina

San Diego

Joshua Tree National Park

Colorado River

Baja California

Flying in from Argentina each March, thousands of swallows arrive in the area of Mission San Juan Capistrano.

The famous Hotel del Coronado, in San Diego, opened in 1888, boasting electric lights in all of its 399 rooms.

Officially designated in 1926, Route 66, which connected Chicago to Los Angeles, was for more than forty years a principal route for Americans on the move.

1873: Cable cars, invented by Andrew Hallidie, begin operating in San Francisco.

1910: The Biograph Company shoots the first movie in Hollywood, located northwest of downtown L.A.

1906: The San Francisco earthquake and fire leave more than half the population homeless.

1890: Thanks in large part to the efforts of naturalist John Muir, Yosemite National Park is created.

1890: Showcasing the bounty of California's mild weather, the Tournament of Roses parade starts in Pasadena.

1st Prize

Dear Grandpa,
At the End of the Oregon Trail Interpretive Center, in Oregon City, we got to see what it was really like to walk more than halfway across America like the pioneers did.
From, Ben

Beginning in Independence, Missouri, the Oregon Trail was the path taken by tens of thousands of pioneers traveling west between 1840 and 1870. It is nearly two thousand miles long.

END OF THE OREGON TRAIL

"I must walk toward Oregon, and not toward Europe. And that way the nation is moving....We go westward as into the future, with a spirit of enterprise and adventure." ~ Henry David Thoreau, 1862

Considered "the Father of Oregon," John McLoughlin helped the early settlers.

His people pursued by U.S. troops, Chief Joseph led the Nez Percés on a thousand-mile journey toward Canada. Finally forced to surrender, he said, "I will fight no more forever."

Mount Hood is a dormant volcano and Oregon's highest peak.

State flower: Oregon grape

OREGON
STATEHOOD 1859
Portland and Mount Hood

Dear Grandma,
Mill Ends Park, in Portland, may be the smallest park in the world. They say it's a home for leprechauns.
Love, Annie

Called the City of Roses, Portland celebrates the Rose Festival for three weeks each June.

State bird: Western meadowlark

The frieze on the Astoria Column, built in 1926, tells the region's early history.

Linus Pauling, who won the Nobel Prize in Chemistry in 1954 and the Nobel Peace Prize in 1962, was born in Portland.

Astoria Column

Haystack Rock, Cannon Beach

alex. we saw hundreds of really noisy sea lions in the sea lion caves near florence.
ben

Astoria
Cannon Beach
Tillamook
Portland
Oregon City
Mount Hood
SALEM
Eugene
Florence
Willamette Valley
Cascade Range
Columbia River
Baker City
Snake River
Pacific Ocean
Coquille River Lighthouse
Crater Lake and Wizard Island
Ashland

A variety of crops are grown in the Willamette Valley, such as peppermint, hazelnuts, and blackberries.

Lumber and Christmas trees are important Oregon products.

Oregon Shakespeare Festival, Ashland

The Space Needle, which has a revolving restaurant at the top, was built for the 1962 Seattle World's Fair.

In the Washington state tartan, adopted in 1991, green represents forests; blue, lakes, rivers, and the ocean; white, the snowcapped mountains; red, apples and cherries; yellow, wheat and grain crops; and black, the eruption of Mount St. Helens.

WASHINGTON
STATEHOOD 1889

Seattle's Space Needle and Mount Rainier

One of the largest Sitka spruce trees is in the Quinault Rain Forest, which is also known as the Valley of the Giants.

Washington ranks first nationally in the production of apples.

State bird: Willow goldfinch

Experience Music Project, Seattle

Experience Music Project, housed in a building designed by Frank Gehry, was founded by Paul Allen, who was also a founder of Microsoft Corporation.

After settlers from the Oregon Trail began to populate this area, negotiations began to move Native Americans onto reservations. Chief Seattle worried about his people, saying, as his words have come down to us, "No bright star hovers about the horizon."

Dear Grandma,
Did you ever have a fish fly by your face? At the famous Pike Place Fish Market, in Seattle, fish sellers sling fish to one another. Fun! Love, Annie

alex. in the san juan islands we learned about the "pig war." look it up! ben

In the 1960s the town of Leavenworth transformed itself into a Bavarian Village.

Leavenworth BAVARIAN VILLAGE WILLKOMMEN

Seattle was named after Chief Seattle.

State flower: Coast rhododendron

Bill Gates, from Seattle, founded Microsoft in 1975. The giant computer software company has its home in Redmond today.

Pacific Ocean
San Juan Islands
Puget Sound
Quinault Rain Forest
Everett
Redmond
Seattle
Leavenworth
Cascade Range
Long Beach
Takoma
OLYMPIA
Mount Rainier
Mount St. Helens
Yakima
Columbia River
George
Grand Coulee Dam
Spokane River
Spokane
Snake River
Walla Walla

Grand Coulee Dam is the largest concrete structure in the United States.

On May 18, 1980, Mount St. Helens erupted, causing 230 square miles of destruction.

In 1916 in Seattle, William Boeing started an airplane company that would become the largest in the world.

Dear Grandpa,
Washington is the only state named after a president. There's even a city here called George, Washington. From, Ben

International Kite Festival, Long Beach

In 1836, near Walla Walla, Narcissa Whitman and her husband, Marcus, founded the first mission in what would become Washington State.

A red wagon that weighs twenty-six tons and has a slide for a handle sits in Spokane's Riverfront Park.

Alaska, the largest state, has the largest national park, national forest, state park, and oil field. It also has the longest coastline of any state.

★ ALASKA ★

Wearing traditional Inupiat parka

STATEHOOD 1959

About one of every sixty Alaskans has a pilot's license. Juneau is the only capital city in the United States that is accessible only by boat or plane.

Eskimo mask at the Sheldon Jackson Museum in Sitka.

Arctic Ocean

Barrow

Russia

Prudhoe Bay

Bering Strait

Seward Peninsula

Nome

The Trans-Alaska Pipeline carries oil eight hundred miles from Prudhoe Bay to the port of Valdez.

Fairbanks

Canada

During the Klondike gold rush of 1897 and 1898, tens of thousands of prospectors flooded into Alaska.

In northern Alaska there are days in the summer when the sun never goes down.

Mount McKinley, also called Denali, is the highest mountain in North America.

Mt. McKinley (Denali)

Wrangell St. Elias National Park and Preserve

Palmer

Anchorage

Valdez

Yukon Delta National Wildlife Refuge

Wood-Tikchik State Park

Skagway

JUNEAU

Tongass National Forest

IT HAPPENED HERE:
In 1942 Japanese forces occupied Attu and Kiska islands. In 1943 the United States recaptured the islands, making the Aleutians the site of the only North American land battles of World War II.

State flower: Forget-me-not

Bristol Bay

Bering Sea

Glacier Bay National Park and Preserve

Sitka

Attu

Kiska

Aleutian Islands

Pacific Ocean

Ketchikan

Totem poles are displayed at Totem Bight State Historical Park and the Totem Heritage Center, both in Ketchikan, as well as in other southeastern communities.

In 1927 thirteen-year-old Benny Benson, of Swedish, Aleut, and Russian heritage, won the territorial flag competition. His design was adopted as the state flag in 1959, when Alaska became a state.

Susan Butcher won the Iditarod four times.

1867

State bird: Willow ptarmigan

The annual Iditarod Trail Sled Dog Race from Anchorage to Nome recalls a 1925 medical mission in which a relay of twenty dog teams carried medicine 674 miles in 127 hours to halt a deadly epidemic in Nome.

alex. we learned two-foot high kick, an inuit ball game. it's hard! ben

Cabbage at the Alaska State Fair, Palmer

Russian Orthodox churches in southern and western Alaska are a reminder of the state's Russian heritage.

Dear Grandma,
Cama! (That means "hello" in Yup'ik.) Veggies get huge in Alaska because of long summer days. I saw a seventy-six-pound cabbage at the state fair in Palmer! Love, Annie

His experiences during the Klondike gold rush inspired Jack London to write about Alaska. The Call of the Wild and White Fang are two of his best-known works.

Totem poles carved by native people of the Pacific Northwest often recount family history and commemorate important people and events.

In the early nineteenth century a Spanish adviser to Kamehameha I began planting pineapples to see how they would fare in Hawai'i.

The third Friday in August is a holiday, commemorating Hawai'i statehood in 1959.

State flower: Yellow hibiscus

Dear Grandma,
The Hawaiian language has beautiful words, like King Kamehameha and humuhumunukunukuapua'a, which has been honored as the state fish. Aloha! (That means "hello" and "good-bye.")
Love, Annie

"It was tranced luxury to sit in the perfumed air and forget that there was any world but these enchanted islands." ~ Mark Twain, 1872

alex. brave annie went surfing with a professional surfer on oahu's waikiki beach. ben

Ni'ihau   Kaua'i

'Iolani Palace, on O'ahu, was the residence of Queen Lili'uokalani until she was overthrown in 1893.

IT HAPPENED HERE: On December 7, 1941, Japanese forces attacked Pearl Harbor, killing 2,390 Americans and bringing the United States into World War II. The USS Arizona Memorial marks the resting spot of the battleship where 1,177 sailors and marines died.

O'ahu   Kailua
Pearl Harbor   HONOLULU
Moloka'i
Haleakalā National Park
Lāna'i   Maui
Kaho'olawe

One of the world's most active volcanoes is Kilauea.

Mauna Kea   Hilo
Mauna Loa
Kilauea
Hawai'i

Waikīkī Beach, Honolulu

Nineteenth-century missionaries built schools and churches, discouraged hula, and introduced the mu'umu'u when they came to Hawai'i.

Missionaries also discouraged surfing, but Duke Kahanamoku, an Olympic swimming medalist, led a resurgence of interest in the sport in the early 1900s.

State bird: Nēnē

★ HAWAI'I ★
STATEHOOD 1959

Mauna Kea Observatory, on the highest mountain of Hawai'i, houses the world's largest optical and infrared telescopes, the Keck I and Keck II.

Hawai'i is the only state made up entirely of islands. There are 132 islands in the Hawaiian archipelago, but only 7 are inhabited.

In 1959 Daniel Inouye, who fought heroically for the United States in World War II, became the first Japanese American elected to Congress.

"The greatest thing I have learned is how good it is to come home again." ~ Eleanor Roosevelt

alex. saw the biggest state and the littlest state, the highest place in the country and the lowest, the place where the pilgrims landed, where the constitution was signed, and where lewis and clark started out. saw where the mississippi begins, where movies got started, and where astronauts get launched. so many cool places. america is great! ben

HOME SWEET HOME

AVOCADOS

★ ★ ★ HOW DID STATES GET TO BE STATES? ★ ★ ★

Throughout this book, in the seal designating the name of each state, there is a date. In the case of the thirteen original states—Massachusetts, Connecticut, Rhode Island, New Hampshire, New York, New Jersey, Delaware, Pennsylvania, Virginia, Maryland, North Carolina, South Carolina, and Georgia—the date indicates when the state ratified the Constitution.

For the other thirty-seven states the date represents when statehood was achieved. Many became states according to a pattern established by the Northwest Ordinance in 1787 and codified by the U.S. Congress: Residents of a territory petitioned Congress for admission to the Union, and after they took certain steps, such as drawing up a constitution, their area was declared a state fully equal to all other states by a joint resolution of Congress.

But other patterns have also been followed. Texas, for example, was not a territory but an independent republic before becoming part of the United States. It joined the Union by way of a congressional resolution that authorized its annexation and also gave Texas the right to divide, should it so choose, into as many as five states. In 1845 the people of Texas approved annexation, and Texas joined the Union. Its citizens have, thus far, been content to remain a single entity.

Another question that frequently comes up when students look at maps of the United States is this: Why do states in the West tend to have more regular shapes than those in the East? The reason is that when Thomas Jefferson considered the unsettled lands northwest of the Ohio River in 1784, he thought they should be surveyed in a rectangular pattern that would permit any landowner to measure his property easily. In 1785 this idea was incorporated into a law establishing a grid that would eventually cover thirty states and influence the way their boundaries were drawn. And so it is that in looking at a map of America in the twenty-first century, we see the vision of a Virginian born in the eighteenth.

This book began with fifty-one large loose-leaf notebooks, one for each state and the District of Columbia. Compilations of information, images, and quotations that my research assistant Elisabeth Irwin put together with my guidance, these notebooks were a valuable resource for Robin Preiss Glasser and me, as were the hundreds of books that we consulted in order to tell the stories of Our 50 States. To try to make sure that we were presenting the most important words and images for every state, we consulted people in every state, and I would particularly like to thank Wayne Allard, Bill Anderson, Ruth Bauer Anderson, Nina Archabal, Frank Atkinson, Tracey Baker, Judy Bittner, Bob Blackburn, Mimi Calver, John Carter, Andrew Cayton, Jim Courter, Virgil Dean, Tom Dyer, Walter Edgar, Richard Engeman, Ted Fehrenbach, Jen Field, Corinne Chun Fujimoto, Michael Gannon, Bill Gardner, Judith George, Brent Glass, Edwin Gleaves, Elbert Hilliard, Carol Hoeffecker, Hamilton Horton, Roger Joyce, William Keleher, Christine Keta, John Kleber, Gary Kremer, Jon Lauck, Barbara Maggio, Thomas Mason, Cathie Matthews, Barbara Mattick, Deborah Miller, Mary Murphy, Merl Paaverud, Kent Powell, Lawrence Powell, Michele Ridge, Guy Rocha, Robert Rupp, Gregory Sanford, John Sears, Todd Shallat, John Sharpless, Earl Shettleworth, Brenda Smith, Kevin Starr, Wayne Temple, Jerome Thompson, Phil VanderMeer, and Bill Youngs.

Robin and I would also like to acknowledge the National Geographic United States Atlas for Young Explorers, to which we have looked for guidance in placing geographical features in Our Fifty States. We also found two series, America the Beautiful, published by Children's Press, and Celebrate the States, published by Benchmark Books, to be useful touchstones.

The Internet is a treasure trove of information on the states, and what follows is a sampling of useful Web sites for those who would like to learn more.

GENERAL
The African-American Mosaic, http://www.loc.gov/exhibits/african/intro.html
American Journeys, http://www.americanjourneys.org/
American Memory, from the Library of Congress, http://memory.loc.gov/ammem/ftpfile.html
The Gilder Lehrman Institute of American History, http://www.gilderlehrman.org/
The National Archives, http://www.archives.gov/
National Museum of American History, http://americanhistory.si.edu/
National Park Service, http://www.nps.gov/
The Smithsonian Institution, http://www.si.edu/
The White House: History and Tours, http://www.whitehouse.gov/history/life/

ALABAMA
Alabama Department of Archives and History, http://www.archives.state.al.us/ts.html
Alabama.gov, the Official Website of the State of Alabama, http://www.alabama.gov/

ALASKA
Alaska History and Cultural Studies, http://www.akhistorycourse.org/
Alaska Native Heritage Center, http://www.alaskanative.net/
Alaska Natural History Association, http://www.alaskanha.org/
State of Alaska Department of Commerce, Community, and Economic Development: Student Information, http://www.commerce.state.ak.us/oed/student_info/student.htm
Statewide Library Electronic Doorway, http://sled.alaska.edu/

ARIZONA
Arizona @ Your Service, Official Web Site of the State of Arizona, http://az.gov/webapp/portal/topic.jsp?id=1164
Arizona Heritage Traveler, http://www.azhistorytraveler.org/templates/index.php
Arizona State Library, Archives, and Public Records: Arizona History, http://www.lib.az.us/archives/azhistory.cfm

ARKANSAS
Arkansas History Commission, http://www.ark-ives.com/
Arkansas Secretary of State: Educational Materials, http://www.sos.arkansas.gov/educational_history_facts.html

The Butler Center for Arkansas Studies, http://www.cals.lib.ar.us/butlercenter/
The Encyclopedia of Arkansas History and Culture, http://www.encyclopediaofarkansas.net/
University of Arkansas Libraries: Special Collections, http://libinfo.uark.edu/specialcollections/default.asp

CALIFORNIA
The Bancroft Library: Reference and Access, http://bancroft.berkeley.edu/reference/links.html
California Historical Society, http://www.californiahistoricalsociety.org/
California History Online, http://www.californiahistory.net/
California State Library, http://www.library.ca.gov/history/cahinsig.cfm
Historical Society of Southern California, http://www.socalhistory.org/
My California, http://my.ca.gov/state/portal/myca_homepage.jsp
San Diego Historical Society, http://www.sandiegohistory.org/
The Virtual Museum of the City of San Francisco, http://www.sfmuseum.org/

COLORADO
Colorado Historical Society: Kids' Page, http://www.coloradohistory.org/kids/kidspage.htm
Colorado State Archives: History FAQs, http://www.colorado.gov/dpa/doit/archives/history/histfaqs.htm
Hewit Institute: Doing History, Keeping the Past, http://hewit.unco.edu/dohist/themes.htm

CONNECTICUT
The Connecticut Historical Society, http://www.chs.org/
Connecticut History Online, http://www.cthistoryonline.org/
Connecticut's Cultural Gateway, http://www.ctculture.org/
Connecticut's Heritage Gateway: Travel, Tourism, and Cultural Resources, http://www.ctheritage.org/links/heritage_links.htm
Connecticut State Library, http://www.cslib.org/
ConneCT Kids, http://www.kids.state.ct.us/index.htm

DELAWARE
State of Delaware: A Brief History, http://www.state.de.us/gic/facts/history/delhist.htm

University of Delaware Library: Internet Resources for Delaware, http://www2.lib.udel.edu/subj/stdc/internet/

DISTRICT OF COLUMBIA
Cultural Tourism DC, http://www.culturaltourismdc.org/
DC.Gov, Government of the District of Columbia, http://www.dc.gov/

FLORIDA
Florida Electronic Library, http://www.flelibrary.org/
Florida Heritage Collection, http://susdl.fcla.edu/fh/
Office of Cultural and Historical Programs, http://dhr.dos.state.fl.us/

GEORGIA
Digital Library of Georgia: Education, http://dlg.galileo.usg.edu/Topics/Education.html?Welcome
Georgia.gov: History and Culture, http://www.georgia.gov/00/channel_title/0,2094,4802_4987,00.html
GeorgiaInfo: This Day in Georgia History, http://www.cviog.uga.edu/Projects/gainfo/dayinhis.htm
The New Georgia Encyclopedia, http://www.georgiaencyclopedia.org/nge/Home.jsp

HAWAI'I
Bishop Museum, http://www.bishopmuseum.org/
The Hawaiian Historical Society: Hawai'i History Moments, http://www.hawaiianhistory.org/moments/moments.html
Hawaii Center for Volcanology, http://www.soest.hawaii.edu/GG/hcv.html

IDAHO
Idaho.gov: History, http://www.state.id.us/aboutidaho/history.html
Idaho State Historical Society, http://www.idahohistory.net/

ILLINOIS
Illinois.gov: Illinois Facts, http://www.illinois.gov/facts/
Illinois Historic Preservation Agency: Learning Online, http://www.illinoishistory.gov/lib/Learn.htm
Illinois State Museum: Online Exhibits and Offerings, http://www.museum.state.il.us/exhibits/index.html?TopicID=10

INDIANA
Indiana Historical Bureau, http://www.statelib.lib.in.us/www/ihb/ihb.html

Indiana Historical Society: Indiana's Popular History, http://www.indianahistory.org/pop_hist/index.html
Indiana State Information Center: About Indiana, http://www.in.gov/sic/about/

IOWA
The Iowa Heritage Digital Collections, http://iowaheritage.lib.uiowa.edu/
State Historical Society of Iowa, http://www.iowahistory.org/

KANSAS
Kansas.gov: Facts and History, http://www.kansas.gov/facts/
Kansas History, http://skyways.lib.ks.us/history/
Kansas History Online, http://www.kansashistoryonline.org/ksh/
Kansas State Historical Society, http://www.kshs.org/

KENTUCKY
Kentucky Department for Libraries and Archives, http://www.kdla.ky.gov/
Kentucky Department of Tourism, http://www.kentuckytourism.com/
Kentucky.gov: Geography and History, http://kentucky.gov/Portal/Category/fac_history

LOUISIANA
About Louisiana: History and Culture, http://www.state.la.us/about_history.htm
Louisiana Secretary of State: All Around Louisiana, http://www.sec.state.la.us/around/all.htm
Louisiana State Museum, http://lsm.crt.state.la.us/

MAINE
Maine.gov: Facts and History, http://www.maine.gov/portal/facts_history/
Maine Memory Network, http://www.mainememory.net/
Secretary of State's Kids' Page, http://www.mainc.gov/sos/kids/

MARYLAND
Baltimore County Public Library: Maryland History, http://www.bcplonline.org/info/history/maryland.html
Maryland Historical Society, http://www.mdhs.org/
Maryland Kids Page, http://www.mdkidspage.org/KidsHome.htm
Maryland State Archives, http://www.mdarchives.state.md.us/

MASSACHUSETTS

The Boston Historical Society and Museum, http://www.bostonhistorical.org/

The Freedom Trail Foundation, http://www.thefreedomtrail.org/home.htm

Massachusetts Archives, http://www.sec.state.ma.us/arc/arcidx.htm

The Massachusetts Historical Society, http://www.masshist.org/welcome/

Mass.Gov, the Commonwealth of Massachusetts, http://www.mass.gov

Museum of Afro-American History, Boston, http://www.afroammuseum.org/

MICHIGAN

Historical Society of Michigan, http://www.hsmichigan.org/

Michigan Department of History, Arts, and Libraries, http://www.michigan.gov/hal

Michigan EPIC, Center for Michigan History Studies, http://www.michiganepic.org/

MINNESOTA

Minnesota Digital Library, http://www.mndigital.org/

Minnesota Historical Society: State Capitol, http://www.mnhs.org/places/sites/msc/

Minnesota Secretary of State Student Page, http://www.sos.state.mn.us/student/

North Star, Minnesota State Government Online, http://www.state.mn.us

MISSISSIPPI

Mississippi Department of Archives and History, http://www.mdah.state.ms.us/index.html

Mississippi History Now, http://mshistory.k12.ms.us/

Mississippi Oral History Project, http://www.usm.edu/msoralhistory/index.htm

Mississippi Secretary of State, http://www.sos.state.ms.us/sos_newhomepage/default.asp

MISSOURI

Discovering Lewis and Clark, http://www.lewis-clark.org/index.asp

The Journals of the Lewis and Clark Expedition, http://libtextcenter.unl.edu/lewisandclark/index.html

Lewis and Clark Across Missouri, http://lewisclark.geog.missouri.edu/index.shtml

The Missouri Heritage Project, http://dese.mo.gov/moheritage/

Missouri Secretary of State: 2005–2006 Official Manual, http://www.sos.mo.gov/bluebook/

MONTANA

Montana Historical Society, http://www.his.state.mt.us/

Mt.gov, Montana's Official State Website, http://www.mt.gov/

Travel Montana, http://www.visitmt.com

NEBRASKA

Nebraska Blue Book Online, http://www.unicam.state.ne.us/bluebook/

Nebraska.gov, the Official Website of Nebraska, http://www.nebraska.gov

Nebraska State Historical Society, http://www.nebraskahistory.org/

NebraskaStudies.org, http://www.nebraskastudies.org/

NEVADA

Department of Cultural Affairs: Discover Nevada History, http://dmla.clan.lib.nv.us/docs/nsla/archives/history/

State of Nevada: Nevada Information, http://www.nv.gov/new_KidsHomework.htm

NEW HAMPSHIRE

State of New Hampshire, http://www.nh.gov/

NEW JERSEY

The New Jersey Historical Society, http://www.jerseyhistory.org/

New Jersey Travel and Tourism: New Jersey History, http://www.state.nj.us/travel/history.shtml

NEW MEXICO

Historical Society of New Mexico, http://www.hsnm.org/

Museum of New Mexico, http://www.museumofnewmexico.org/

New Mexico Office of the Governor, http://www.governor.state.nm.us/index2.php

New Mexico Tourism Department, www.newmexico.org/index2.php

NEW YORK

Columbia University Libraries: New York City and Its History, http://www.columbia.edu/cu/lweb/eguides/amerihist/nyc.html

I Love NY, the Official New York State Tourism Website, http://iloveny.com

New York State, http://www.ny.gov/

Researching New York, http://nystatehistory.org/researchny/

NORTH CAROLINA

The North Carolina Collection: North Carolina History Sources, http://www.lib.unc.edu/ncc/nchistory.html

The North Carolina Encyclopedia, http://statelibrary.dcr.state.nc.us/nc/cover.htm

North Carolina Historic Sites, http://www.ah.dcr.state.nc.us/sections/hs/default.htm

The State of North Carolina Kids Page: North Carolina History, http://www.secretary.state.nc.us/kidspg/history.htm

NORTH DAKOTA

North Dakota Tourism, http://www.ndtourism.com/

State Historical Society of North Dakota, http://www.state.nd.us/hist/index.html

State of North Dakota, http://www.nd.gov/

OHIO

Ohio History Central, http://www.ohiohistorycentral.org/

Ohio Public Library Information Network: Discover Ohio, http://www.oplin.org/main.php?Id=63&msg

Ohio Secretary of State, http://www.sos.state.oh.us/

OKLAHOMA

A Look at Oklahoma, http://www.otrd.state.ok.us/StudentGuide/default.html

Oklahoma Historical Society, http://www.ok-history.mus.ok.us/

Oklahoma's History, http://www.ok.gov/osfdocs/stinfo2.html

OREGON

End of the Oregon Trail Interpretive Center: History Library, http://www.endoftheoregontrail.org/histhome.html

Oregon Blue Book, http://bluebook.state.or.us/default.htm

Oregon Historical Society, http://www.ohs.org/

PENNSYLVANIA

ExplorePAhistory.com, Your Gateway to Pennsylvania, Past and Present, http://www.explorepahistory.com/

The Historical Society of Pennsylvania: Philadelphia History, http://www.hsp.org/default.aspx?id=111

National Constitution Center, http://www.constitutioncenter.org

Pennsylvania General Assembly, http://www.legis.state.pa.us/

Pennsylvania Historical and Museum Commission, http://www.phmc.state.pa.us/

RHODE ISLAND

Office of the Secretary of State, Rhode Island, http://www.sec.state.ri.us/

State of Rhode Island General Assembly, http://www.rilin.state.ri.us/

SOUTH CAROLINA

SC.GOV, the Official Web Site of the State of South Carolina, http://www.sc.gov/

South Carolina Encyclopedia, http://www.scencyclopedia.org/

SOUTH DAKOTA

South Dakota State Historical Society, http://www.sdhistory.org/

South Dakota State Library, http://www.sdstatelibrary.com/

State of South Dakota, http://www.state.sd.us/

The Weekly South Dakotan, South Dakota Treasure Chest for 4th-Grade History, http://www.sd4history.com/

TENNESSEE

Tennessee Department of State: Tennessee Blue Book, http://www.state.tn.us/sos/bluebook/

The Tennessee Encyclopedia of History and Culture, http://tennesseeencyclopedia.net/

Tennessee.gov, the Official Web Site of the State of Tennessee, http://www.tennesseeanytime.org/index.html

TEXAS

The Handbook of Texas Online, http://www.tsha.utexas.edu/handbook/online/

Texas Beyond History, the Virtual Museum of Texas' Cultural Heritage, http://www.texasbeyondhistory.net/index.html

Texas Historical Commission: Texas Trivia and Fun Facts, http://www.thc.state.tx.us/triviafun/trvdefault.html

Texas State Library and Archives Commission: Archives and Manuscripts, http://www.tsl.state.tx.us/arc/

UTAH

Utah Collections Multimedia Encyclopedia, http://www.uen.org/ucme/

Utah History Encyclopedia, http://www.media.utah.edu/UHE/

Utah History to Go, http://historytogo.utah.gov/

Utah State History, http://history.utah.gov/

VERMONT

The University of Vermont Libraries: Wilbur Collection of Electronic Vermontiana, http://library.uvm.edu/about/specialcollections/scev.html

Vermont Division for Historic Preservation, http://www.historicvermont.org/

Vermont Historical Society, http://www.vermonthistory.org/

Vermont Secretary of State's Kids' Page, http://www.sec.state.vt.us/kids/kids_index.htm

VIRGINIA

Jamestown Rediscovery: History of Jamestown, http://www.apva.org/history/

Virginia General Assembly: Capitol Classroom, http://legis.state.va.us/cap_class/cap_class_welcome.html

Virginia.gov: Facts and History, http://www.virginia.gov/cmsportal/visiting_883/history_3815/index.html

Virginia Historical Society, http://www.vahistorical.org/

WASHINGTON

Access Washington: State Facts, http://access.wa.gov/statefacts/index.aspx

Center for the Study of the Pacific Northwest, http://www.washington.edu/uwired/outreach/cspn/

HistoryLink.org, the Online Encyclopedia of Washington State History, http://www.historylink.org

Washington Secretary of State: Washington History, http://www.secstate.wa.gov/History/

Washington State Digital Library Resources, http://digitalwa.statelib.wa.gov/

WEST VIRGINIA

West Virginia Division of Culture and History: History Center, http://www.wvculture.org/HISTORY/history.html

WV.gov: All About West Virginia, http://www.wv.gov/sec.aspx?pgID=19

WISCONSIN

Wisconsin.gov: Frequently Asked Questions—State of Wisconsin, History/Culture, http://www.wisconsin.gov/state/core/faq_wisconsin_history_culture.html

Wisconsin Historical Society, http://www.wisconsinhistory.org/

Wisconsin State Legislature, http://www.legis.state.wi.us/index.htm

WYOMING

State of Wyoming: About Wyoming, http://wyoming.gov/about.asp

Wyoming State Historical Society, http://wyshs.org/index.htm

Wyoming State Museum, http://wyomuseum.state.wy.us/

★ ★ ★

SONG CREDITS

SHRINE
LIVE-THRU TREE
...CALIFORNIA

Thru Tree,

Stanton Hall,

Everglades

Floating in the
Great Salt La...

American Gothic house, Eldon,
site of Grant Wood's famous painting

Fiesta San Antonio

Plymouth Rock

...e Ticonderoga

Waikiki Beach, Honolulu

Atlantic City

Four Corners

SIMON & SCHUSTER BOOKS FOR YOUNG READERS ★ An imprint
of Simon & Schuster Children's Publishing Division ★ 1230 Avenue of the
Americas, New York, New York 10020 ★ Text copyright © 2006 by Lynne V. Cheney ★
Illustrations copyright © 2006 by Robin Preiss Glasser ★ All rights reserved, including the
right of reproduction in whole or in part in any form. ★ SIMON & SCHUSTER BOOKS FOR YOUNG
READERS is a trademark of Simon & Schuster, Inc. ★ Book design by Jessica Sonkin and Dan Potash ★ The text for this
book is set in Seria Bold. ★ The illustrations for this book are rendered in black ink, watercolor washes, and colored pencil. ★ Manufactured in the United
States of America ★ 10 9 8 7 6 5 4 3 ★ Library of Congress Cataloging-in-Publication Data ★ Cheney, Lynne V. ★ Our 50 states : a family adventure across
America / Lynne Cheney ; illustrated by Robin Preiss Glasser. — 1st ed. ★ p. cm. ★ Summary: "Each of the fifty states is represented by important people, ideas, and
events in the history of the United States"–Provided by publisher. ★ ISBN-13: 978-0-689-86717-0 (hardcover) ★ ISBN-10: 0-689-86717-4 (hardcover) ★ 1. U.S. states—
Juvenile literature. 2. United States—History, Local—Juvenile literature. 3. United States—History—Juvenile literature. 4. United States—Description and travel—Juvenile
literature. I. Preiss-Glasser, Robin. II. Title. III. Title: Our fifty states. E180.C47 2006 ★ 973—dc22 ★ 2006015281 ★ First Edition

A portion of Mrs. Cheney's proceeds from this book is being
donated to charity.

BERKELEY

Dotty's Nut...
...ER TAFFY

...ER TAFFY

QUAHOG
1st Place...

The International
Quahog
Amat... Bake-...

...or of Dia...
Day